The Smashing Pumpkins

Mellon Collie and the Infinite Sadness

Transcribed by ANDY ALEDORT & HEMME LUTTJEBOER

Very Special Thanks to Andy Aledort for his assistance.
Billy Corgan's "Guitar Geek U.S.A."
Articles reprinted by permission of *GUITAR WORLD*

Cover Art: JOHN CRAIG
Book Design: ODALIS SOTO
Project Manager: AARON STANG
Music Editors: COLGAN BRYAN & AARON STANG

Smashing Pumpkin's Billy Corgan presents a

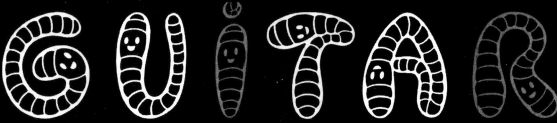

highly personal, alternative take on guitar

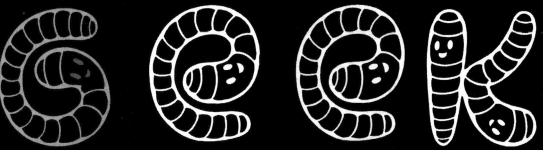

playing in this, the first of six exclusive

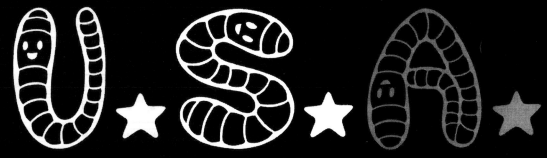

columns for Guitar World.

BY BILLY CORGAN

Photo By Lisa Johnson
Typography By Steven Cerio

'D LIKE TO begin this first installment of my new column with a statement: *There is no right or wrong.* What you read here represents just one person's views on the crazy, frustrating thing we call music. You have every right to disagree with me on any or every point—in fact, doing so will help to clarify your own point of view.

When it comes to guitar playing, the true judge of what's "good" and what's "bad" is the player himself. Some people say Frank Zappa, for example, was an awful guitarist. Others maintain he was a genius. Some people, like Steve Lukather, think I'm a terrible guitar player. Others disagree. The point is that everyone is entitled to his

BILLY CORGAN

or her own opinion, and you shouldn't let someone else's taste influence you too much. (Although I would say that if "Hold The Line" was the best rock riff *I'd* ever written, I think I'd keep my mouth shut.)

Guitar playing, in and of itself, does not mean a whole heck of a lot. But guitar playing within the context of great music and great songs *is* a big deal. If you look at the guitarists who are most noted for their playing ability, you will find that their reputations are inextricably tied to the great songs they have written, or at least reinterpreted in their own unique ways. We appreciate the guitar-playing skills of Eric Clapton, Jimi Hendrix, Jimmy Page and others within the context of their songs. The downfall of the Yngwie Malmsteen school of guitar playing, which focuses almost solely on technical proficiency, has occurred because ultimately, no one really gives two shits about guitar playing in and of itself, except maybe other guitar players.

These days, there are three-chord punk bands enjoying huge popularity, and no one can tell me that their style of playing—which doesn't even involve guitar solos—is somehow less influential than guitar playing based on virtuosity. When you get right down to it, the guitar playing of Green Day's Billie Joe Armstrong has a lot in common with that of a Seventies guitar hero like...Ted Nugent. Both have been very influential because their styles are *very accessible.*

And there we come upon the magic word. My intention with these columns is to present an accessible approach to guitar playing that emphasizes individuality as expressed through songwriting. Among the topics I hope to discuss are:
1. Finding your own style. (There is no reason to play the guitar just to sound like everyone else.)
2. Using the guitar as a songwriting tool.
3. Developing a creative approach to guitar sound for both studio and live situations.
4. Understanding the important differences between recording and live performance. This topic will also include an exploration of the many possibilities the studio affords you, such as overdubbing, as well as a look at the ever-present problem of replicating "studio magic" in a live situation.
5. Dealing with six-string hopelessness: why bother playing guitar at all when true geniuses like Hendrix have already taken the instrument to such seemingly unsurpassable heights?
6. The almighty riff (the topic of this month's column).

EVERY GREAT ROCK song has a great riff, be it a single-note melody or a chordal-based sequence, and that's probably what makes it a great song. Like a great frontman, a really good rock riff should have a hypnotic, star quality. A great riff can take you

over; you might find yourself playing it repeatedly for 10 minutes. There's something about it that makes you want to indulge in it.

If I were to define the word "riff," I would say that it's an instrumental part of a song that gives the song a certain identity, defines it in some way. Led Zeppelin's "Whole Lotta Love" riff is a textbook example of this: the minute you hear it, you know what song it is. In my own experience, I've found that really complicated riffs, although they may sound great on their own, don't make for the best songs. Simplicity, it seems, is a key ingredient; once again, just listen to "Whole Lotta Love." That riff also has another very important attribute: you can sing over it. This is crucial, because while a powerful riff will often open up a song, it often will not be the riff that continues to drive the song along.

"Siva," from our first album, *Gish,* had one of those riffs [see **FIGURE 1**] that let me know immediately that I had a *song,* even though I had yet to work out all the parts. James Iha adds to the riff by playing a contrasting sequence [**FIGURE 2**]. That riff sounded like my *band*—it had instant identity—and it got my blood

going right away. There was something about it that was so distinctive that it made a lot of other songs I'd written seem wimpy and weak by comparison. Since then, I've always tried to find that weird marriage of a great riff and a song that fits with the riff. The "Siva" riff crystallized everything I was trying to do with the band. It had power and immediacy, and the song seemed to write itself *around* the riff.

When I wrote "Siva," I was working in a record shop, and I used to bring an acoustic guitar with me to work. When no one was in the store, I'd just sit behind the counter and play. So, this was a riff that I wrote on acoustic, keeping in mind that I would transfer it to loud, heavily distorted guitar later. It was buzzin' in my head!

Almost a reverse-case scenario occurred with the song "Today," from *Siamese Dream.* I had all of the chords and the melody, but no opening hook. At that point, we just started the song with the verse chord progression [Eb-Bb-Ab], which in and of itself is catchy because of the melody. I knew I had to come up with some sort of opening riff. Then, out of the blue, I heard the opening lick note for note in my

BILLY CORGAN

head [**FIGURE 3**]. That's the state of mind I've trained myself to be in: I'm always looking for the *guitar hook*. When I added the opening riff, it completely changed the character of the song. Suddenly, I had a song that was starting out quiet and then got very loud. I could start to hear the shifts in the song as it progressed. I knew that I was going to bring that riff back in for emphasis, and I knew where I could do that.

In the realm of songwriting, you really have to mine the territory and search for good riffs. Both of these examples show that heaviness is not the only thing that makes for a good riff; of far greater importance is the context within which the riff is used. To me, the best rock riff writer right now is Diamond Darrell of Pantera. At the other end of the sonic spectrum is the Edge from U2, who plays completely stylized parts which propel the songs.

It would be ridiculous for me to claim that each riff I write is great, or that it is in no way derivative of music that has influenced me. Unfortunately, the guitar is an instrument that has been explored so thoroughly that it's hard to come up with a catchy, instantly recognizable riff that sounds totally new. That brings me back to Diamond Darrell: he's taken the down-tuned D thing (where the low E string is tuned down a whole step to D) to a new extreme. He's developed his own language around it, and he's playing some incredible things.

When I find that I can't seem to escape the shackles of what's already been done, or if I feel that I'm locked into a "traditional" way of thinking, I turn to rhythm guitar. Ultimately, that seems to open up infinite possibilities—far more than just sitting around noodling. Another option is to play the bass, which seems to push my writing in a more rhythmic direction. "I Am One," from *Gish*, is an example of a song that has a pretty decent guitar riff, but a killer bass riff to support it. Here's the bass riff [**FIGURE 4**], and here's the guitar part that goes over it [**FIGURE 5**].

You can start with the high-falutin' idea of sitting down and writing the ultimate rock riff, but if you can't do that, or if you can't find something that sounds unique and different, you should go backwards—to the very nature of what makes music work, which is rhythm. Using a drum machine, playing the bass, or even just toying with different chords in different rhythms opens up new possibilities that you may not otherwise discover.

Another way to inspire yourself to come up with good riffs is to use effects, and to try different tunings. The great thing about effects is that they change the way you hear the guitar, thereby changing the way you *react* to the guitar. The most mundane licks can turn into something completely different with the right effect. Phasers, flangers, fuzzboxes and especially delay units will all

inspire new ideas. David Gilmour has done some incredible things with delays in Pink Floyd.

For the song "Starla," from *Pisces Iscariot*, I had a riff [FIGURE 6] which didn't really do much for me. Then, I ran it through a fuzz (which gave it a drone-y sound and added some different harmonics), and panned it back and forth in time with the song. Soon, I started to hear an orchestration for the song. The effects inspired the arrangement, even though I didn't end up using the original effects on the final version of the tune.

Different tunings, like effects, will make the guitar seem like a whole new instrument. James wrote "Mayonnaise" [Siamese Dream] after just screwing around with tunings until he came up with something he liked (Eb, Bb, Bb [same octave], Gb, Bb, D) . Using this tuning, he stumbled across an Ebsus2/Cm/Ab chord progression, which ultimately shaped the song. For the record we're working on now, we're tuned down a half step for everything. This alone is altering the way we play and how our songs will sound.

You must force yourself away from what you know into territory that is often uncomfortable, and occasionally disappointing. There is as much potential in songwriting as you are willing to mine, but it doesn't always come easily. You've got to work at it. I wish you the luck of the Metal Gods. ●

GUITAR GEEK U.S.A.

BY BILLY CORGAN

SEARCHING FOR STYLE

with my good eye closed

WE HAVE A saying in Smashing Pumpkins: "By hook or by crook." Which means, "no matter how it gets done, just get it done." Often, when we're arranging a song, we'll reach a point where it becomes boring to us or the arrangement is stale. At that point, we'll take the arrangement and totally fuck with it. After all, the worst thing that can happen is that we'll go in a complete circle and end up right where we started.

There's no *harm* in taking this approach, you shouldn't be afraid of the unknown. In fact, I think that fear of the unknown is one of the main reasons people tend to associate themselves with one specific music genre. My attitude is, why be only one kind of band? Why be just a rock band? Why be just a punk band? You are you, and you can do whatever you want to do, so long as it's within your limitations. And those imitations are always changing. The fact that Jimi Hendrix and Jimmy Page seem to have done it all already doesn't fucking matter. The notion of the past as somehow representing certain limitations for you today is bogus. I used to have so much reverence and respect for the great accomplishments of past artists that it stiffled me into thinking, "Gee, I could never do any of this." But the whole point of making music is that it's an expression of who you are, be it angry, happy or sad. If you can somehow reflect that musically, you've achieved something.

UNDER THE INFLUENCES

EVERYONE IS INFLUENCED by the past, whether they want to believe it or not. When we start to play an instrument, we look to what we admire and what moves us, and we naturally gravitate in that direction. For the beginning guitarist, studying the work of others is a very important method of learning the instrument. But you'll lose your way if you start trying to think and play exactly like one of your mentors. I've often said of my own music that I don't always like what I do, but that at least it reflects my perspective.

The purpose of trying to find your own style is to discover how to express who you are via your instrument. What you need to address is how do I take those same, dumb three chords and turn them into a language all my own?

If you're a 16 year-old heavy metal kid, you probably can't image that one day you'll be writing soft, ballady love song. But that's what happened to me! I've grown to appreciate that part of myself, but the fact of the matter is, it's something that I never, ever anticipated. It just hap-

pened because I allowed the sentimental, "wimpy" side of myself to emerge.

I think there is a correlation here to Jimi Hendrix' *Axis: Bold As Love* album. Jimi made the decision to make a beautiful album of love songs, instead of writing more macho, psychedelic material like "Purple Haze" and "Foxy Lady." This was not a calculated ,mercenary move; nor was it a particularly popular one. I'm sure that although there were plenty of forces pushing against his making this type of album, he felt it necessary to do so. If you listen to *Axis,* you hear someone searching for new sounds and feelings. To me this represents a great accomplishment, and we should thank Jimi for having the guts to record what was in his heart.

There have been many people in my life who've tried to tell me what I am and what I'm not. For instance, I was told that I couldn't sing. Obviously, I didn't listen to that. There are better singers, and better guitar players, but I have achieved a certain degree of success with the abilities that I have. I think this success stems from my having respect for whatever talent I do have... call it God-given, inherent or whatever, I did not plan out the course of my evolution as a musician; I didn't grow up thinking that I'd be part guitar player, part singer, part *anything*. Those things happened on their own.

Though we naturally gravitate towards the things we admire and respect, those things don't necessary reflect who we really are. When I was young, I was influenced by the gun-slinger/Yngwie/Eddie Van Halen school of guitar. In the end, though, that's not where my heart guided me; in any case, I probably don't have the talent to be that kind of guitar player. There came a day when I realized that even if I practiced eight hours a day, every day for five years, I still might not be that good. I had to make a realistic evaluation of what I was, and it involved a lot of soul searching.

When I was 18 years old, I reached a pivotal point. I was out of school, and I decided I was going to play music. I had long black hair, I looked weird, I acted weird, and I played a heavy metal style of guitar that was not popular with my friends. Everybody I knew who *looked* like me played like Robert Smith of the Cure. And everybody who played like me had big poodle hair! Finally, I decided that the guitar playing angle was useless, and that I would start working on my songwriting. Then I began using my knowledge of the guitar to help me with the writing. My initial songwriting efforts were based on my ability to play interesting little guitar things. Today, I can pretty much do whatever I need to do on the

guitar, relative to what's most important to me. I still can't do Yngwie-esque reverse sweep arpeggios, or whatever those runs are that I could never figure out, but I don't really have a need to play that stuff anyway.

PRACTICING

Practicing usually falls into one of two polar camps: the technique-oriented, "I must never make a mistake" camp and the punk rock camp, which holds that practice just makes you sound like everybody else. For me, the actual truth lies somewhere in between these two extremes. There have been times with my band when I felt the musicianship wasn't proficient enough, and this is the way I explained my point of view to them: You should never let your technical limitations prevent you from achieving your goals. If you have the artistic vision of playing something *grand,* don't let your lack of technical ability keep you from getting there. The most important thing is what you're trying to say, and you need to work on whatever it is that will enable you to express yourself eloquently.

In terms of my own playing, I've always had a crazy vision of a lot of dynamic changes, so it's always been important that I have some technical proficiency. I never would have been able to execute something like "Geek U.S.A." from *Siamese Dream,* without having practiced the guitar. You can't be a bad guitar player and play a song like that. But if all you care to play are punk rock/barre chord kinds of songs, you'll be able to do that within a year of practicing for one hour a day.

At some point in your development, it's important to acquire a basic understanding of music theory. Most people who are musical have an intuitive understanding of the structure of music. After I'd been playing for about three years, I went out and got some books that explained the basic scales and their relationships, because I felt I couldn't develop any further without finding out why I was trying to put the notes together in the way that I was. Learning the mechanical reasons for how music works opened up other doors that I hadn't anticipated. There are certain aspects to musical language that, once understood, will help you to express yourself. This brings you into the realm of a kind of fearlessness, and an ability to embrace music as a whole. As you learn the language, you learn to speak your own unique dialect. ●

CompuServe members can download audio files to this lesson from the Guitar World File Library (GO GUITAR).

GUITAR GEEK U.S.A.

BY BILLY CORGAN

CompuServe members can download audio files to this lesson from the Guitar World File Library (GO GUITAR).

SONG COMPOSITION AND ARRANGING

IN THIS MONTH'S column, we're going to look at the relative importance of guitar and vocal melodies, making the most of your band's instrumentation and understanding the different roles that your guitar plays as a lead, rhythm and ensemble instrument.

The first thing to address when writing a song is, what is your purpose? Are you in a band with no singer, and you'd like to write a song that's good to solo over? Or do you want to write a song with vocals *and* solos? Before trying to write a song, you should try to have a clear sense of purpose in mind.

In writing for Smashing Pumpkins, I sometimes try something known as *creative visualization*: before playing a single note, I try to imagine what *kind* of song I'd like to write—what it is I'd like to get across in the music. Am I trying to create a quiet, peaceful kind of vibe, or am I looking for a heavy metal barnburner? The goal I set for myself will have a huge influence on how I approach the guitar.

Let's assume that you've already developed something of a style, and have already written some riffs. Where do you go from there? It has always been my approach to prevent the riff from killing the song. In other words, the riff should ultimately be used only in such a way that it serves to bolster the song. It's the bigger picture—the song as a whole—that's most important.

"Geek U.S.A." *(Siamese Dream)* is a good example of this "song first" way of thinking. Originally, the intro riff was like this (**FIGURE 1**). We played it this way for a while, but it never really took off and it sounded too Black Sabbath-y. What ultimately happened proved to be a good argument for observing the commandment, "Never throw a riff away." For if you keep playing it, and keep fucking with it, sooner or later you might find a use for it. This rejected riff lingered in my head for about a year. Finally, I was just fucking around with it one day, and I played it like this (**FIGURE 2**). Our drummer, Jimmy Chamberlin, started playing a syncopated rhythm under-

FIGURE 1

FIGURE 2

FIGURE 3

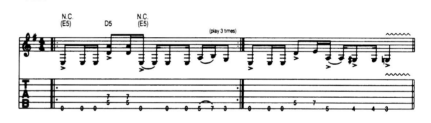

FIGURE 4

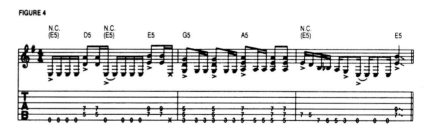

FIGURE 5

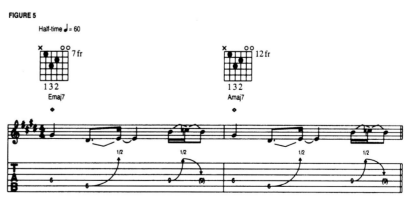

FIGURE 6

Double time ♩ = 120

FIGURE 7

neath, and, *boom*, that was it!

I now had to decide whether this was going to be the riff I was going to sing over. I ruled against this, so I needed to find a variation to play under the vocals. I then wrote this (**FIGURE 3**). During the process of writing a song, you will often create complimentary riffs which essentially are spin-offs of the original riff. This is where working with a vocalist—or being a vocalist yourself—will prove integral to the development of the song. Ultimately, it is the vocals that determine the "success" of the song.

The next step in writing "Geek U.S.A." was to ascertain whether I could use the initial riff for the chorus. It didn't work out, so then I had to write *another* part. The chorus riff (**FIGURE 4**) is a spin-off of the verse riff. I now had the main riff, the verse riff and the chorus riff, which led me back to the initial riff shown in **FIGURE 2**. But instead of just repeating it verbatim, I overdubbed high single notes and a couple of little riffs on top of it. Even though the additions are minor, I used these little melodic guitar figures to carry the song's arrangement along.

When I got up to about the two-minute point, I wanted to do something that would change up the song and send it in another direction. After two minutes, a song this heavy ceases to have any *dynamic* impact. You can't play it any louder, and you can't play it any faster. My trick is go in the opposite dynamic direction, which we in the band refer to as a "reset." We reset the dynamics by quieting down the song, which serves to increase the impact of it getting loud and heavy again. So, at that

two-minute point we start to play this (**FIGURE 5**). The funny thing is, that little insert was actually a *different* song idea. Remember: Never throw out a riff.

After all these shifts in dynamics, the song then kicks back into ultra-heaviness. This new surge of adrenaline gave me a few choices of where to go, and in this case I opted for a guitar solo to jack up the song.

After the solo section ends, I follow with a vocal section that I wrote thinking, "What can I sing over that will sustain the full momentum and weight of the song without killing everything that I've set up?" I wrote this ascending chordal figure (**FIGURE 6**) specifically to address my needs at that point of the song. Initially, I was going to play a crazy solo during that section, but, while we were in the studio, I decided that a light, contained part was more appropriate. That line of thought led me to this descending figure (**FIGURE 7**) which is played over the ascending chordal figure. What I've done here compositionally is use the technique of *contrary motion* to elevate the song's dynamics.

What is clearly illustrated is that "Geek U.S.A." was *completely* spawned on the guitar. It may not be the most melodic song ever written, but it's a *motherfucker* guitar song. I use the guitar throughout the song to bring the dynamics up and up and up.

When we were done recording the song, it was a minute and a half longer than the version released on *Siamese Dream*. I had to look at the song as a whole and edit it down. The guitar solo section, for example, was originally a bit longer, but when I stepped back and

looked at the whole picture, I realized that the solo was the least important thing.

Another very important point to make about arranging is that guitarists should cultivate an understanding of the other instruments they're working with. When I was a teenager, I'd make demos on my four-track and play the bass parts myself. My father came over to me one day and said, "You play the bass like a guitar player. You've got to sit down and listen to bass playing on records and learn how the instrument functions in the music." This has proved to be an invaluable lesson, not only in terms of songwriting, but in terms of my guitar playing, too.

It's very important to understand *why* a drummer goes to his ride cymbal on the chorus, or why, during a verse, a drummer will push the hi-hat halfway open. Going outside of my little guitar head and understanding why the other musicians play *what* they play has been extrememly valuable in terms of learning about how these instruments interlock. Focusing on these things has only helped me to further understand what it is I want to do with the guitar. In the context of rock, I cannot stress enough how important it is to understand the function of your instrument in the pursuit of creating powerful, effective arrangements. ●

CompuServe members can download audio files to this lesson from the Guitar World File Library (GO GUITAR).

GUiTAR Geek U.S.A.

BY BILLY CORGAN

THE ELEMENTS OF TONE

YOUR TONE HAS a lot to do with how people react to your playing, and your music as a whole. It is as important as the quality of a singer's voice or the accent with which he or she delivers a particular lyric. Many guitarists fail to realize that every aspect of the equipment they use affects their sound, and therefore how they are perceived as an artist. The type of guitar—the wood it's made of, whether it has a rosewood or maple fretboard—the amp, the strings, the pick, the pickups, the effects and the length of your cord all play important roles.

With so many possible gear combinations to chose from, there is only one way to find sounds that appeal to you: *experimentation*. Only experimenting will show you that slight variations in your basic set-up will yield drastically different, and often welcome, results.

Listed below are the essential ingredients that combine to create a guitar sound.

GUITARS

Most electric guitars are based on basic designs created by Gibson and Fender. Few guitarists seem to feel equally comfortable with both designs. Gibsons produce a fat round sound, while Fenders have a more cutting tone. I had never played a Fender Stratocaster until the day that I bought one, but the second I picked it up, I immediately felt like, "This is *it*. This is the sound I've always been looking for." I wished that I had done more experimenting with different guitars, because I would have started playing a Strat much earlier. You really need to try lots of different guitars to find the right one. Avoid getting fixated on one particular instrument simply because one of your heroes plays one.

Once you find a guitar design that you're comfortable with, don't just settle on the first instrument of its type that you come across. Mass-produced guitars are often inconsistent. If you walk into a music store and play five guitars of the same model, one will probably be much better than the others, so play as many as possible. Also, be open to the possibility of buying a used instrument, or even an obscure, no-name guitar, if it's the one that really feels and sounds right to you.

PICKUPS

It's very hard to determine which pickups are best for you, because it's unlikely that you can afford to go out and buy five different sets and try them all in your guitar. A good alternative is to bring a guitar you like to a music store, then compare its sound with similar guitars that are fitted with different pickups. I did this with my Strat, which is how I determined that I liked the sound of Lace Sensor pickups. In essence, I'd found the right blend between the best of both worlds; the cut of a Strat and the bottom end of an SG. They're right at home producing hugely overdriven sounds without generating a shrill top end. After I tried a few guitars with Lace Sensor pickups, I decided to try them in my guitar, and they worked out well.

AMPS

Experimenting with different amps is one of the hardest things for a guitarist to do. It's virtually impossible to walk into a music store and crank up *one* amp, let alone a bunch of them. I recommend that young guitarists with a lack of amp experience buy rack-mountable amps and pre-amps because their sounds are generally very consistent and easy to tailor to different applications. I used an ADA MP-1 preamp for all of *Gish*. I'd written the songs on that unit, and I couldn't imagine them being played any other way.

If you end up with a tube amp, make sure the tubes are working properly. Also, if possible, experiment with different power tubes. I'm a huge fan of using KT-88's in my Marshall. Most people prefer EL-34's, but I hate them. The *Gish/Siamese Dream* guitar sound has so much to do with KT-88's, which add a round, fat bottom to my sound.

Before buying *any* amp, be nosey. Talk to as many guitarists as you can, get different opinions and see what other people like and don't like. I've always done that, and it's always been helpful.

PEDALS

As fun, inexpensive and radical-sounding as pedals can be, their presence in your signal path will usually decrease the overall quality of your sound. If you can, run your effects through your amp's effects loop instead of sticking them in-line, where they will really wreak havoc on your tone.

Sometimes, though, a nice lo-fi pedal is just what you need. When we did *Siamese Dream*, I developed a technique of plugging my Big Muff pedal into the low sensitivity input of a 100-watt Marshall JCM 800, with the master volume on full and the preamp volume barely on at all. To me, the Electro-Harmonix Big Muff produces the ultimate super-gain *VROOOM* sound. Live, however, a Big Muff doesn't give you enough definition. I just keep experimenting with different combinations of pedals—and guitars—to get the ideal sound.

Some of the other distortion boxes I use are the Fender Blender, which generates the most saturated, harmonic-laden sound you can imagine. When it's turned all the way up, it sounds like the end of the world! I also have a wah/fuzz that looks as if it must have been made by Uni-Vibe. Finally, the nasal, squeezed-up lead tone that I use so often—as on "Pissant," for example—I ripped off from Michael Schenker! I used an Electro-Harmonix Micro-Synthesizer and some unknown fuzz pedal, plus an MXR Phase 100.

PICKS, STRINGS & PATCH CHORDS

Most people seem to be unaware of how much their strings affect their sound. I find that the guitar sounds much better when it has relatively new strings. When the strings are *brand* new, however, they usually sound too bright for me, so I play on them for an hour or so before a show. When Smashing Pumpkins are on tour, we have to change our strings for *every* show. The sweat from just one gig will *completely* change their sound for the worse. Old strings lose all of their clarity and brightness, and, worse, will not intonate correctly, so your guitar will be out of tune on different parts of the neck. When this occurs, the strings *must* be changed—don't just wait until they break!

Your string gauge also has a drastic effect on your tone. If you play very heavy, metal-type riffs, you should probably go with a set that's slightly heavier than a standard rock gauge—.052 to .010, for example. For more all-purpose rock guitar styles that involve a lot of soloing and string bending, I recommend .009-.042, which I use.

Even those guitarists who change their strings regularly often neglect to put sufficient effort into their pick selection, perhaps because it takes a great deal of experimentation to find the perfect gauge. Even though we're talking tenths of millimeters here, the effect a given pick will have on your playing is enormous. Texture is also an important consideration: some picks will slip out of your hand more easily than others. Personally, I prefer a heavy, thin pick because it provides me with the right combination of control and power to create the gain I want. You will actually *play* better when you find the right pick, so take your time and explore what the market has to offer.

As far as patch chords are concerned, I've often heard that your signal loses 1db of gain for every 10 feet of cable you use. For years, I used a 30-foot cord when I played live, and couldn't understand why my guitar didn't sound as good as when I played at home, where I used a much shorter cable. The loss of db created by a long cord can make a huge difference in your sound. Again, you need to experiment with different lengths and types of cords, and find what works best for you.

Searching for the perfect gear recipe to suit your tastes is an endless, evolving process. If you buy a better amp, you may notice how shitty your guitar is, and vice versa. I've already spent thousands of dollars in pursuit of the perfect guitar sound, which I'm sure I'll never completely

GUITAR GEEK U.S.A.

BY BILLY CORGAN

GUITAR OVERDUBS

SOME PEOPLE ARE averse to overdubbing because they view it as a "politically incorrect" act. Their view is that overdubbing is not "honest"; that it's cheating, pompous and allows the artist to hide behind production techniques. I disagree. When you are faced with making a permanent recorded representation of a song, why not endow it with the grandest possible vision? Also, I feel that the electric guitar vocabulary has been so thoroughly explored that without "guitar production" techniques like overdubbing, it's extremely difficult to create a sound that's at all unique or new.

The notion of overdubbing guitar parts has always appealed to me. I was experimenting with layering guitar tracks long before I ever set foot in a real recording studio. Early on, I overdubbed by using two cheap tape machines. Then I graduated to a four-track. Every step of the way, I was trying to find different ways to present the guitar—anything to expand the language and find a new voice.

At some point, I decided not to be afraid to take chances, and to record the songs any way I could think of. I'd do anything to the guitar's signal in the name of finding something different, be it in sticking it in a Jello mold, or whatever. Ultimately, all this experimentation helped me to find things I didn't know existed: chord combinations, the way seemingly non-related guitar parts worked together, etc.

For our first album, *Gish,* I did a handful of overdubbing, but on the second record, *Siamese Dream,* I took overdubbing as far as I could, even though I knew that the overdubs would be difficult to recreate when we performed the songs from the album in a live setting. I also knew that some of the songs would be virtually *impossible* to recreate in concert. But in the end, I had faith that we'd be able to present these songs live in a different but equally effective way.

"Soma," from *Siamese Dream,* is a good example of a song with extreme overdubs. The song was originally supposed to have only two distinct guitar parts throughout, just like it would have when we played it live. I got the idea of adding different guitar overdubs from the way *(Smashing Pumpkins' rhythm guitarist)* James Iha and I were playing our respective parts together: during the intro, we were playing different voicings in slightly different cadences, which created a weird kind of *flow.* That sound inspired me to build the song subtly as it progressed, and to embellish the B-E-G chord progression from which it barely strays.

In the intro, James' rhythm part is like this **(FIGURE 1),** to which I added this melody **(FIGURE 2).** To me, the song didn't sound that interesting with just two guitars playing their respective parts, so I began looking for subtle ways to embellish the arrangement. One of my first thoughts was to create a "spacey" atmosphere, I wanted the listener to feel as if the song began in a grand, expansive space, and then to have the music shrink back down to something more immediate. The idea was to evoke the experience of hearing someone from across a large expanse, and then to suddenly have them be right in your face. To widen the sonic landscape on the intro I used delay and reverb effects on two tracks of guitars playing arpeggios, creating the illusion that there are dozens of overdubbed guitars.

At the beginning of the first verse (1:00) is a guitar overdub that sounds like a bubbly spaceship noise; that was a patch on an Eventide harmonizer. There's no change in the notes or the music, but I achieved a subtle change in the feeling of the music with the use of this odd sound effect. Then, on the downbeat at 1:28, I added an acoustic guitar for just one chord, and this served to give the song a little "lift." I'm always looking for ways to bring the song from Point A to Point B to Point C without having it lose momentum, and I'll do whatever I can to serve that purpose.

At 2:26, I brought in a piano to create some contrast with the guitar parts. Then, at the guitar solo section at 3:10, I recorded 14 different tracks of E-Bowed acoustic guitar, compressed and EQ'd them, and then mixed them down to two-track stereo to create one big mass. (For those of you unfamiliar with the E-Bow, it's a device invented in the Seventies, made from an electromagnet that can make a guitar oscillate—along the lines of what happens when a note feeds back. The resultant sound is akin to the bowing of a violin. Guitars with "sustainer" pick-ups use very much the same mechanism.) The melodies I played were all improvised, but were intended to fit together in some sort of way. What ended up happening was that a certain number of the guitars created a base, and then one or two rode over the top and created a prevalent melody.

Obviously, it's impossible to recreate that exact sound live with only two guitarists. We compensate by using some delays and other effects to generate a vibe similar to the recording's. To recreate the E-Bow section, I use a backwards patch on the Eventide Ultra-Harmonizer, which does well in creating a similar effect. There is about a half-second delay between when I actually play the notes and when the effected signal comes out sounding backwards, so I need to anticipate that small lag time as I'm playing. On the album, the dynamics are extremely subtle, whereas live, the dynamic shifts are more pronounced.

It doesn't bother me that we can't recreate some of our album tracks exactly, because when I go to see a band, I like to be surprised. I might know their record inside out and backwards; that is all the more reason I'd want to hear the song played differently. I like to be moved in a way that the record can't move me. That's why I encourage you to never lock into one specific thought about a song. Be open, and let the song itself show you where to go. ●

FIGURE 1 ♩. = 00

B E G

let ring

FIGURE 2

B E G

GUITAR GEEK U.S.A.

BY BILLY CORGAN

INSPIRATION

Inspiration is a funny thing, because there are times when you are completely at a loss. You feel like you are not special, that you have nothing to say, and that everything you play is a bunch of shit, blah, blah, blah. When you hit that point, you have to let go. You can try so hard to reach something that you end up pushing it farther away. At those times when I'm at a loss, I force myself to remember that music is not the only thing that exists in this world. Sometimes, you just have to put the guitar down, instead of throwing it against the wall.

You can sit around and wait for God to intervene, but moments of clarity and understanding—those moments of pure inspiration—are very rare. Most of the time, you have to mine your creativity, you have to search for it. That's where having an awareness of who you are, how you feel, and what you want in this world is completely crucial. If you want to be a pop star, be a pop star. If you'd rather sit in your room and play the guitar all day, that's great, too. There is no right or wrong way to explore and share in the great mystery that is music.

Inspiration can come from any one of many different sources. "Spaceboy," from *Siamese Dream*, began with this basic chordal riff (**FIGURE1**). I was thinking, "Why am I writing a song like this?" The answer was that at that point, I was supposed to be writing *rock* songs for the album; the last thing I needed was another quiet acoustic song. As I continued to mess with the riff, it occurred to me that I was writing about something that had to do with a certain kind of alienation, an "out-of-touch"-ness." I began to think about my brother, and the fact that he and I share a certain identity by virtue of the similar experiences we had growing up. I felt there have been handicaps in my life that reflect the handicaps he has experienced in his. Suddenly, I had stumbled upon feelings and thoughts that moved me, and the song kind of wrote itself.

In and of itself, "Spaceboy" doesn't seem to be anyone's favorite song. Our producer, Butch Vig, didn't think it was an album track, and the band didn't think so, either. But, yet, the spirit of the song—what it meant to me, and what it ended up being about—made it worth putting on the album. This is a good example of where inspiration turned just another song into something that I'm proud of. Of course, if I

assessed "Spaceboy" on the criteria of "Was it a hit song?," the answer is no. Did it have a video? No. Do people cite it as their favorite song? No. Do they scream for it at concerts? No. But does it mean something to me? Yes. And would I do it again? Yes.

The things that are obvious are easy to see. The day after I wrote "Today," my manager heard it and said, "It's a hit," and I guess in a way, it was. The suc-

FIGURE 1   "Spaceboy" ♩ = 56

cess of "Disarm" was no mystery to anyone, either. "Spaceboy" doesn't have the same qualities as those songs; it's different, and that's what I like about it. It grew from a unique kind of inspiration.

So many of us refuse to acknowledge, tolerate or appreciate that there is other music out there than what is hurled at us by MTV and the radio, and that there are other reasons to play music besides trying to make a lot of money. Just because you dislike a certain kind of music doesn't make it bad. There was plenty of music that I thought sucked when I was 14, but, by the time I was 19, I loved it.

I've learned as much about music from things that don't appeal to me as I have from things that do. I'll ask myself, "What is it that everybody likes about this music?" For example, I used to hate jazz; I thought it was a bunch of sophomoric people wanking off, just to show how well they could play their instruments. For the most part, I was wrong about that. I always hated country music, too; I thought it was about beating your wife and drinking too much. Sometimes it is about that, but not usually. I realized that there was a whole history of country music that was amazingly rich, and rock and roll was in part born out of that. There's an entire history of classical music, blues, soul and r&b to be studied and all kinds of other things that are incredibly vibrant and powerful.

Often, I'll turn to music that is very removed from what I'm trying to do as a source of inspiration. I've been blown away by the power of [*Mississippi Delta*

bluesman] Son House's music. He was someone that had been forgotten about; when he re-emerged in the Sixties, he hadn't played for 20 years, but he still was able to record albums of incredible power, beauty and dignity. Unfortunately, most people have never even heard of him.

Reading interviews with musicians that I respect has also been very valuable. Finding out what has influenced and inspired them has, in turn, inspired me to go back to those same sources. When Stevie Ray Vaughan first came out, he was quickly painted as a Hendrix clone. But, if you listen to Stevie Ray play, you can tell that he not only listened to Hendrix, he listened to the same things that inspired Hendrix, such as Muddy Waters, Howlin' Wolf and Albert King. And, within the fairly limited context of 12-bar blues, Stevie had his own personality—and he kicked ass.

Neil Young is someone who has never done what he "should" have done—he's always gone in the opposite direction. He's a great example of someone who has followed his muse, and chased it in a big circle. It took him 20 years to come back around to where he started, but when he did, he had new things to say, most likely as the result of his explorations. The fearlessness and adventurousness he has shown throughout his career has always been very inspirational to me.

Remember, when inspiration is not there, don't be afraid to try *anything*. Sometimes, I'll try tuning the guitar ten different ways just to see what happens. The worst thing that can happen is that you get nothing out of it, and you end up in the exact same place as you started. Be open to anything. Divine inspiration is a tiny part of trying to be a musician and only one out of a billion is a Beethoven. If you are passionate about it, though, you will uncover the talent that is inside you. But you have to work at it. You have to search. The easy thing to do is to say, "What is everyone else doing?," and then do the same thing. We've all been guilty of that. But, ultimately, it's all for naught if you are not willing to throw yourself out into the unknown and be yourself. ●

MELLON COLLIE AND THE INFINITE SADNESS

The piano part has been arranged for solo guitar. The following chord frames show the basic chord shapes used in the guitar arrangement and can also be used to strum along with the piano.

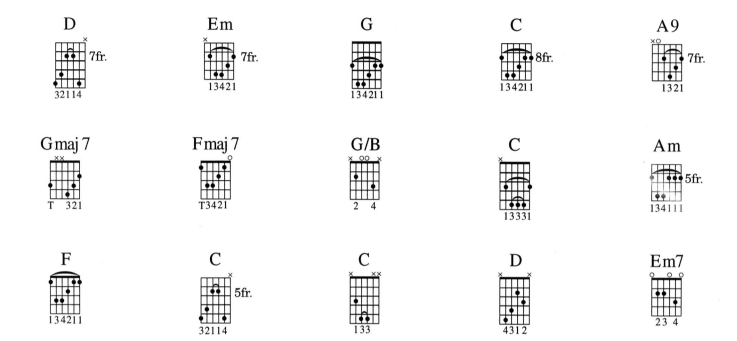

MELLON COLLIE AND THE INFINITE SADNESS

Words and Music by
BILLY CORGAN

Tune down 1/2 step:
⑥ = E♭   ③ = G♭
⑤ = A♭   ② = B♭
④ = D♭   ① = E♭

Moderately slow ♩ = ca. 69

14

w/Synthesized strings

JELLYBELLY

The guitars in this song are tuned to "dropped D"– the ⑥ string is tuned down a whole-step to "D". With this tuning, the basic three note power chord on the bottom three strings can be played with one finger (see the chord frames below), making faster power chord riffs like the intro figure easy to play. To match the recording, tune whole guitar down one half-step.

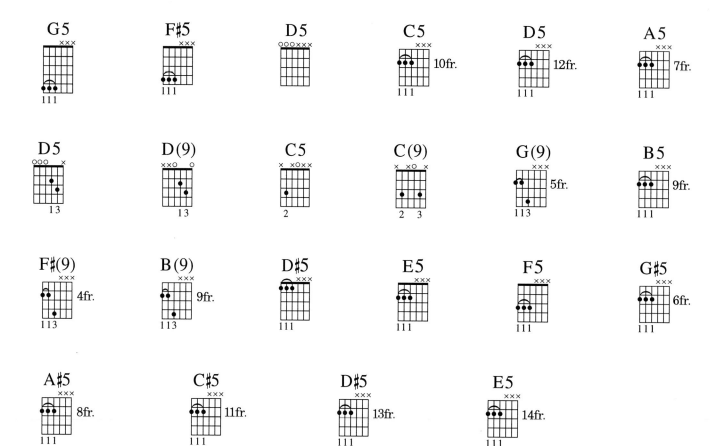

JELLYBELLY

Tune down 1/2 step:
"Dropped D" tuning
⑥ = D♭   ③ = G♭
⑤ = A♭   ② = B♭
④ = D♭   ① = E♭

Words and Music by
BILLY CORGAN

Moderate rock ♩ = 116

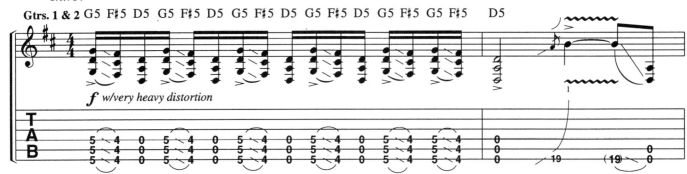

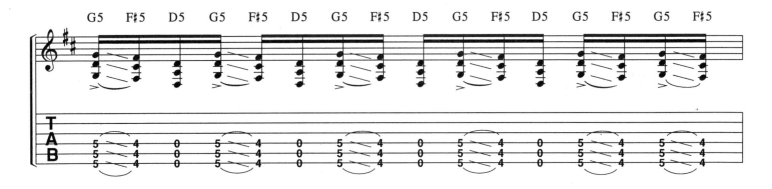

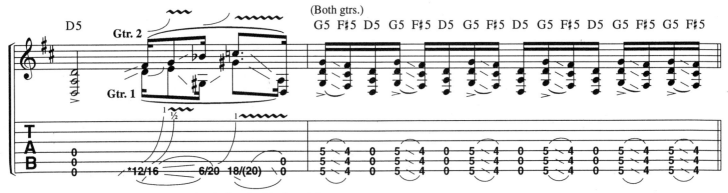

*Gtr. 1 tabbed on left, Gtr. 2 tabbed on right.

18

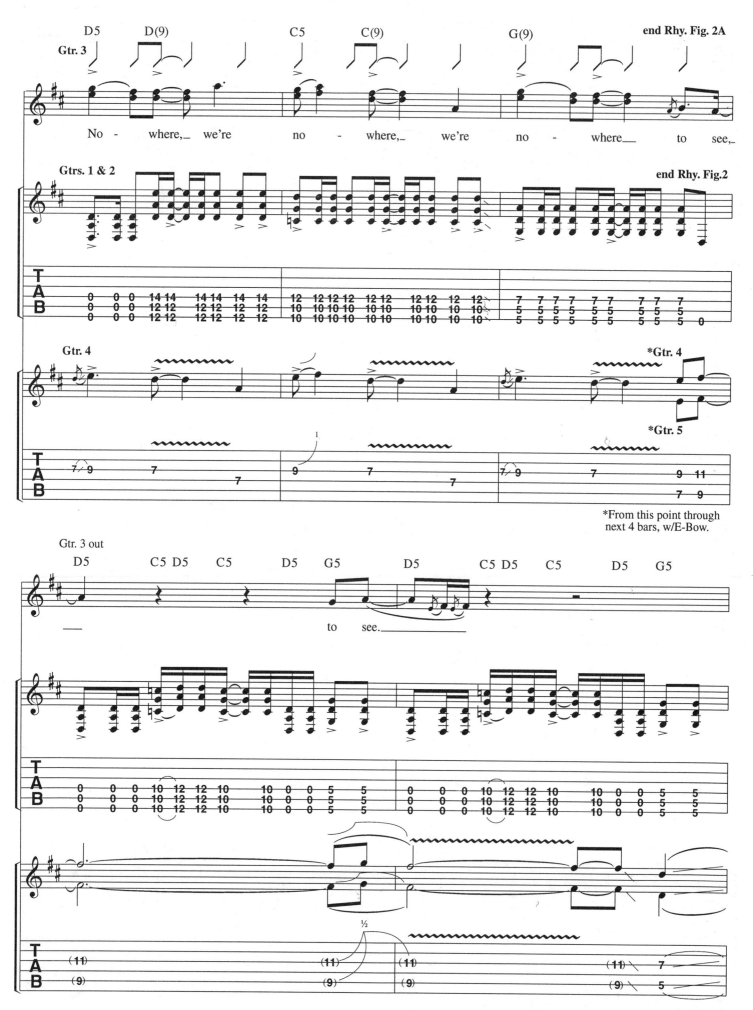

*From this point through next 4 bars, w/E-Bow.

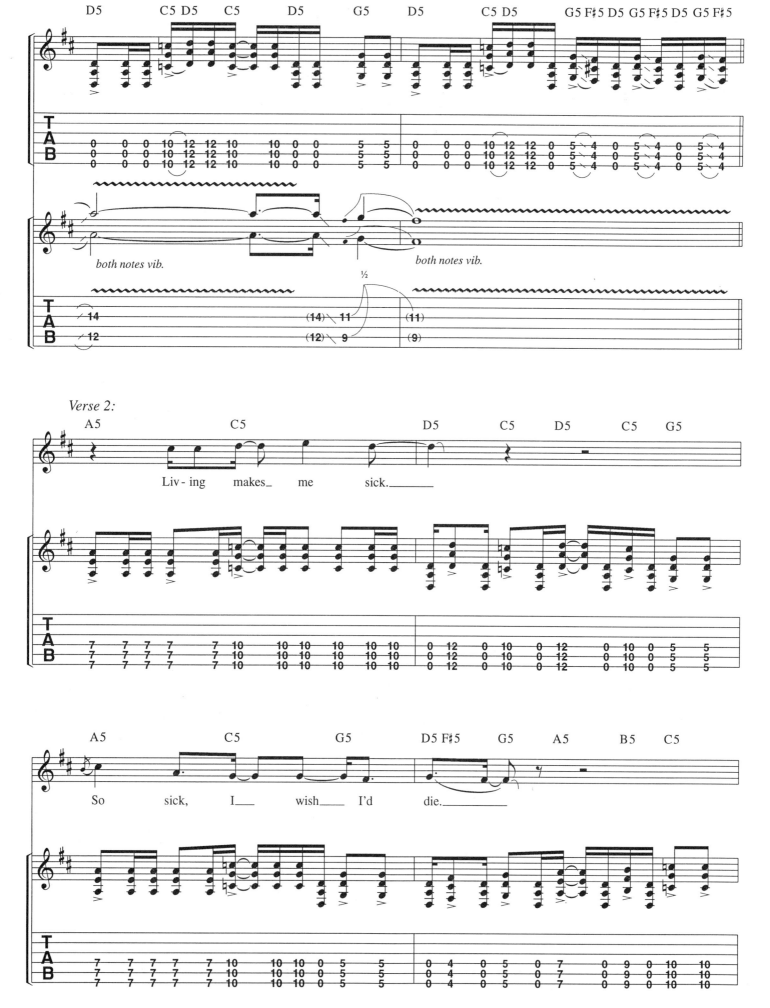

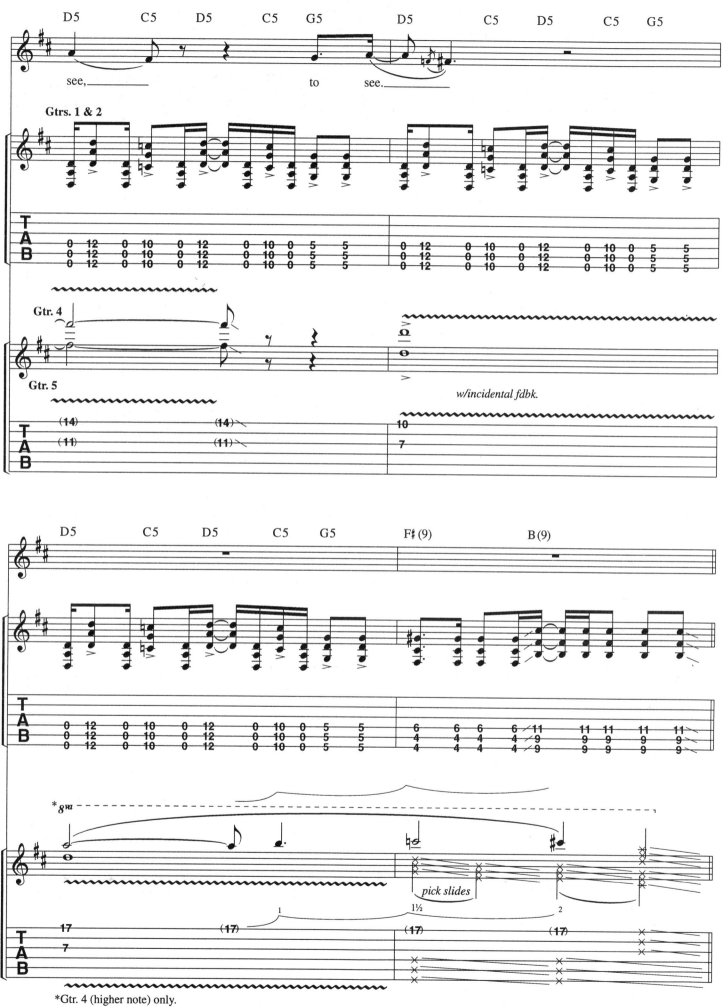

24

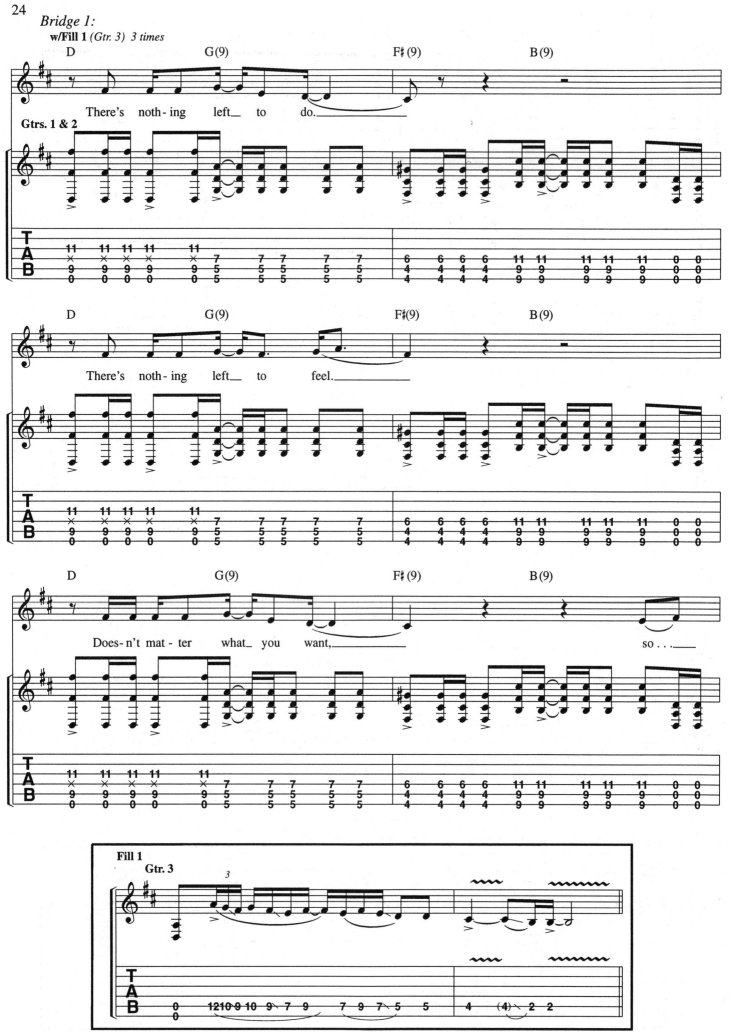

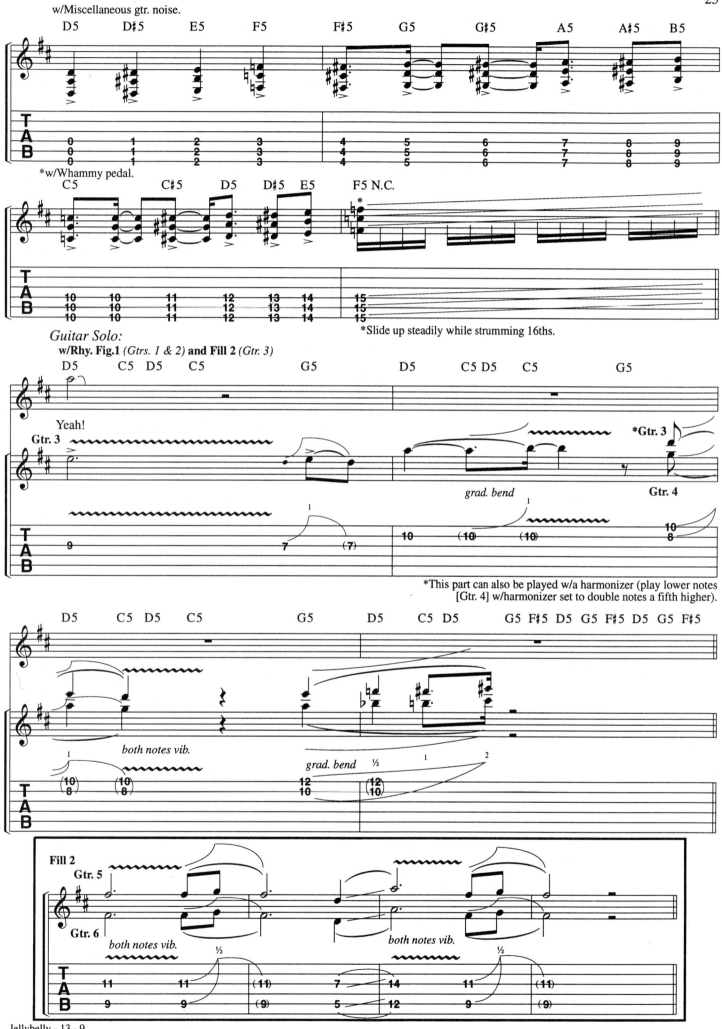

Jellybelly - 13 - 9
PG9602

26

Bridge 2:

*w/wild gtr. noises (overdubs).

*w/whammy pedal.

Yeah!_____

poco rit.

Freely

TONIGHT, TONIGHT

G

21   3

Gsus

23 4

Em

23

Em(♭6)

21 3

C(9)

3 2 4

G/B

2   3

Dsus2

23

G/C

3

G/D

3

Dsus/F♯

T   123

Am

231

C

32 1

TONIGHT, TONIGHT

Words and Music by
BILLY CORGAN

Tune down 1/2 step:
⑥ = E♭   ③ = G♭
⑤ = A♭   ② = B♭
④ = D♭   ① = E♭

Moderately up tempo rock ♩ = 152

Intro:
w/Synthesized strings   **Rhy. Fig. 1**
Gtrs. 1 & 2 *(Elecs.)*

34

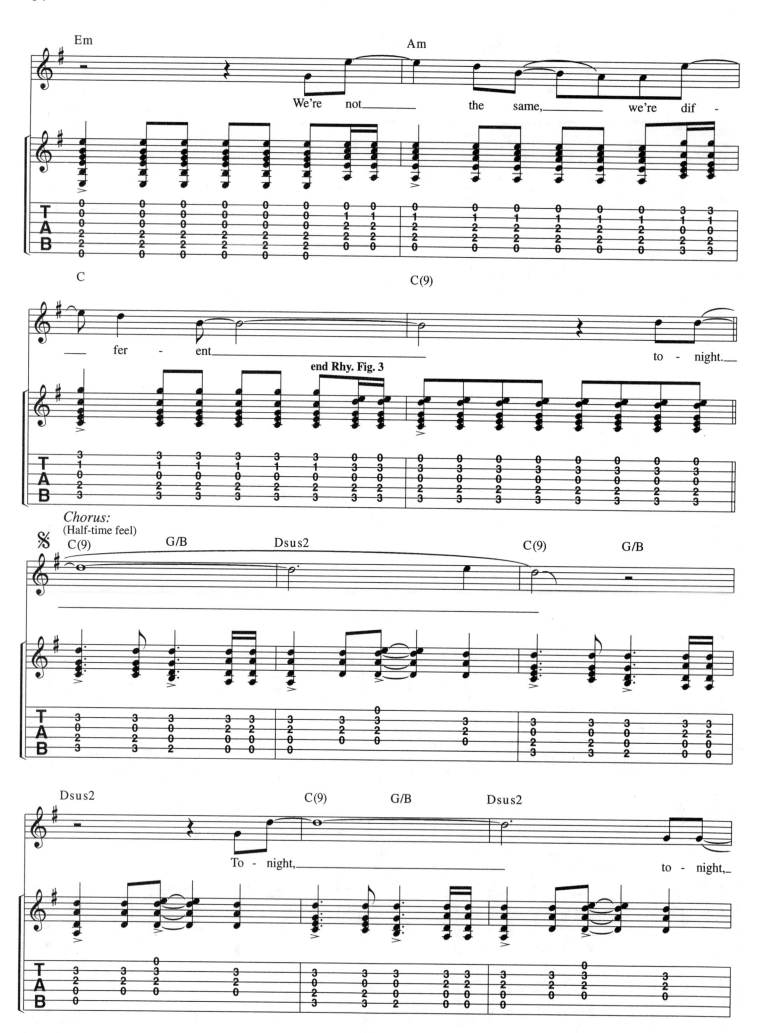

36

Tonight, Tonight - 8 - 6
PG9602

HERE IS NO WHY

Words and Music by
BILLY CORGAN

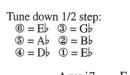

Tune down 1/2 step:
⑥ = E♭ ③ = G♭
⑤ = A♭ ② = B♭
④ = D♭ ① = E♭

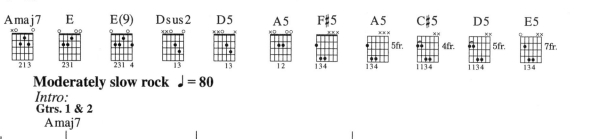

Moderately slow rock ♩ = 80

Intro:
Gtrs. 1 & 2

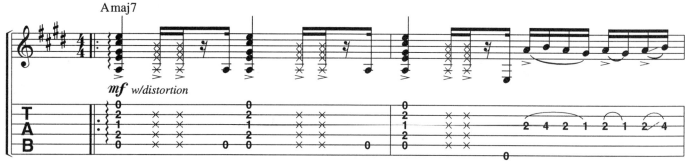

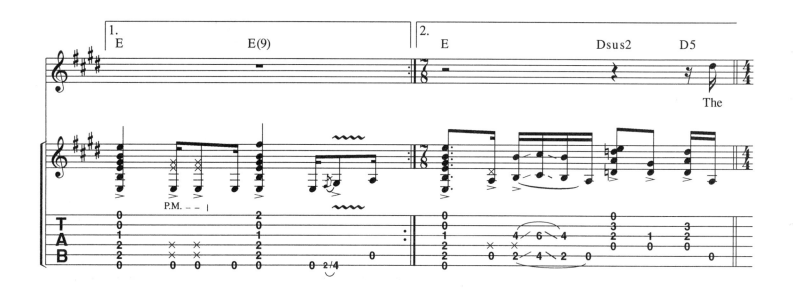

Verse 1:

use-less drag___ of an-oth-er day,   the end-less drags___ of a death___ rock boy.___

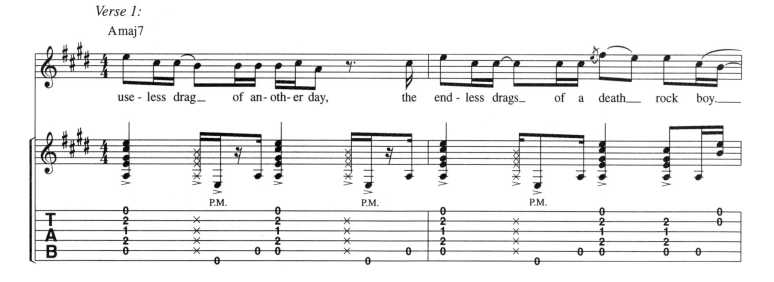

Here Is No Why - 9 - 1
PG9602

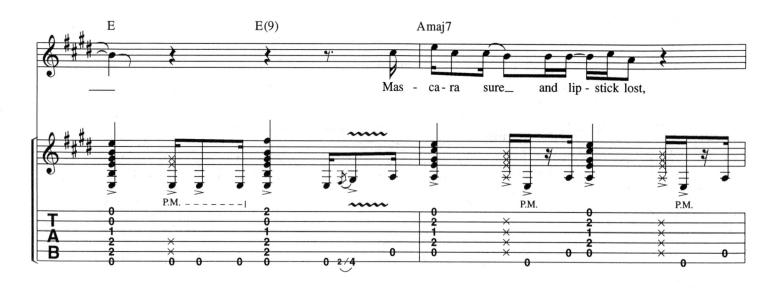

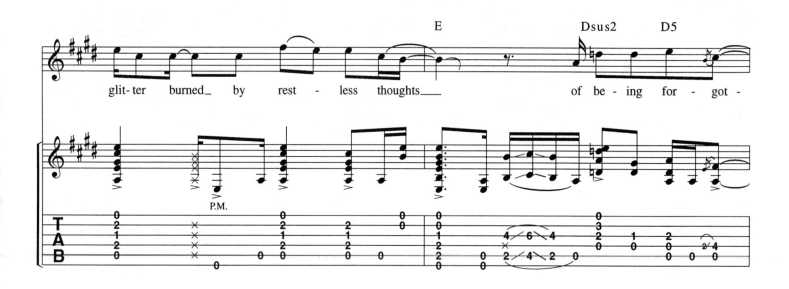

Chorus 1:

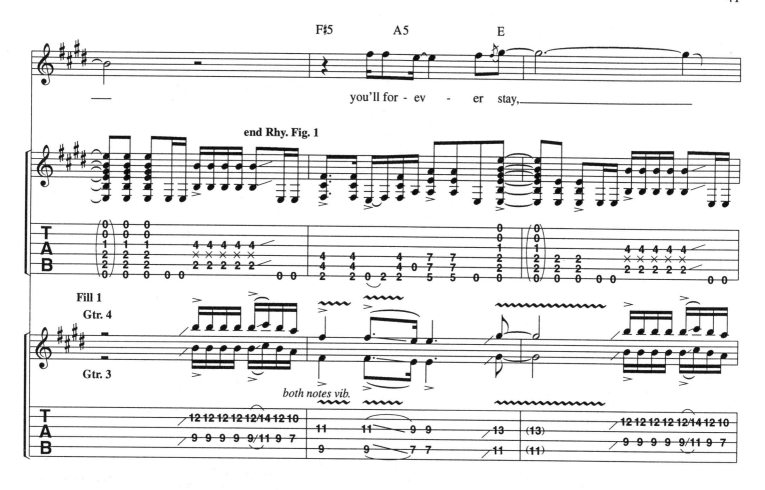

Verse 2:

Some - where, he pulls his hair___ down___

o - ver a frown - ing smile.___ A hid-den dia-mond you can-not find. A

se-cret star___ that can - not shine___ o - ver to you.___

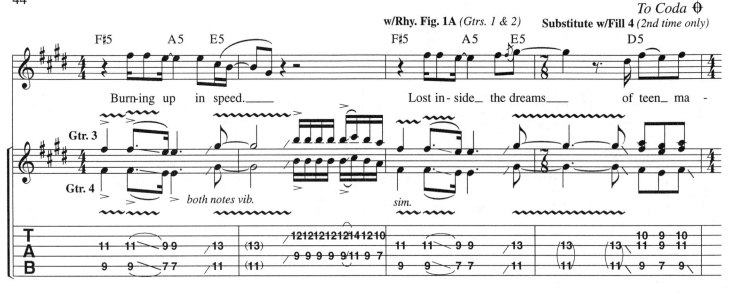

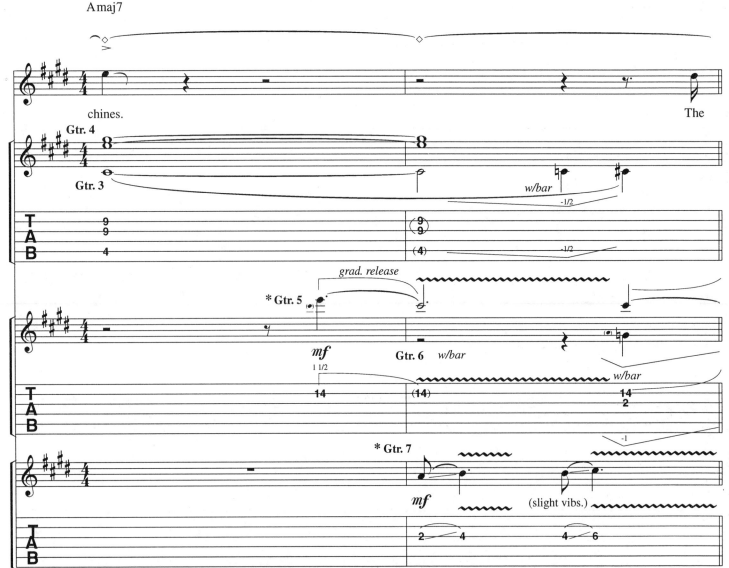

* The "melodies" played in this section are produced by feedback, E-Bow (a magnetic device), slide guitar and conventional picking. This is an arrangement of many guitar overdubs.

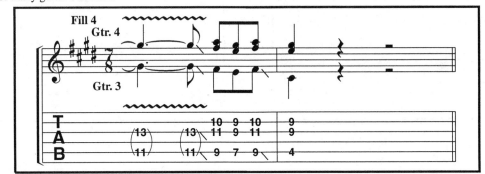

Verse 3:
w/additional overdubbed gtr. effects.

use - less drags,_ the emp - ty days. The lone - ly tow - ers of long_ mis - takes. For -

got - ten fac - es and fad - ed loves. Sit - ting still_ was nev - er e - nough!_

*Notes on B (2nd stg.) &D (4th stg.) played by Gtr. 7. Notes on G (3rd stg.) played by Gtr. 8.

Guitar Solo:
w/Rhy. Fig. 2 *(Gtrs. 1 & 2) 4 times*

*Doubles Mellotron melody.

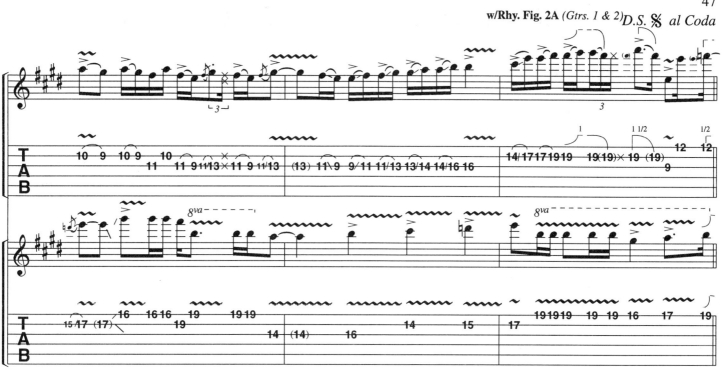
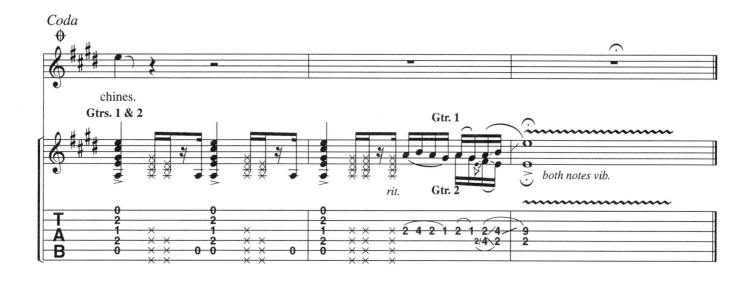
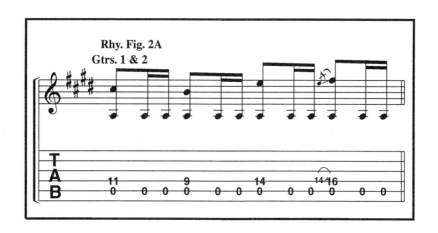

48

BULLET WITH BUTTERFLY WINGS

The Verse to this song features an interesting guitar part. Essentially the chord remains constant (B5) but the bass note of the chord keeps shifting. The bass note is indicated with a slash: B5/G, B5/E and B5/A.

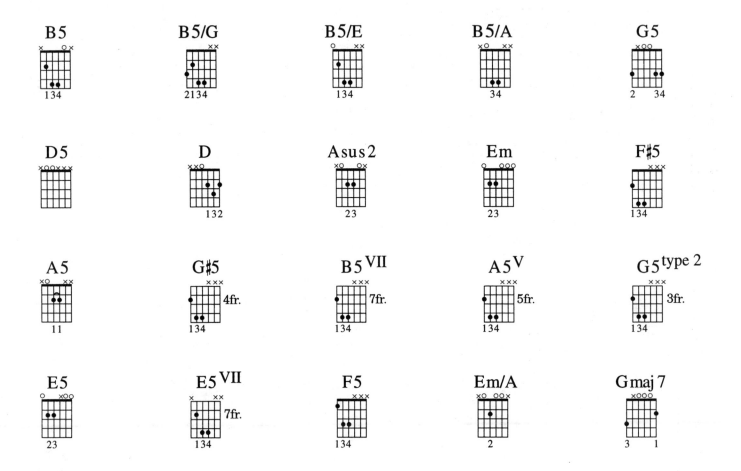

BULLET WITH BUTTERFLY WINGS

Tune down 1/2 step:
⑥ = E♭ ③ = G♭
⑤ = A♭ ② = B♭
④ = D♭ ① = E♭

Words and Music by
BILLY CORGAN

Moderate rock ♩ = 120

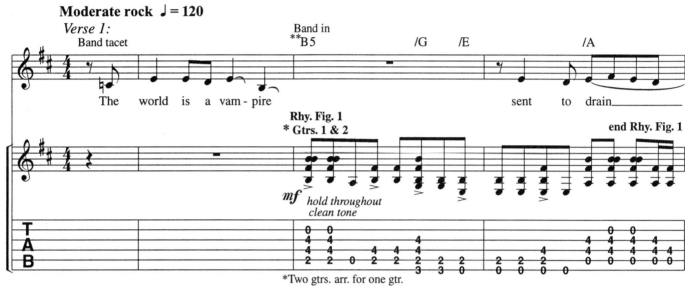

*Two gtrs. arr. for one gtr.
**Hold B5 throughout, changing only the bass notes.

w/Rhy. Fig. 1 *(Gtrs. 1 & 2) 6 times*

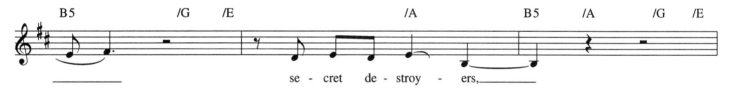

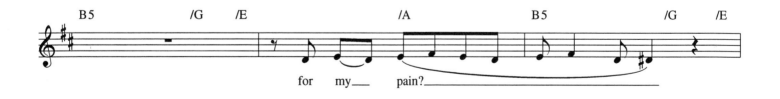

52

*Vibrato whole chord.

Bullet With Butterfly Wings - 9 - 5
PG9602

54

Bullet With Butterfly Wings - 9 - 7
PG9602

56

TO FORGIVE

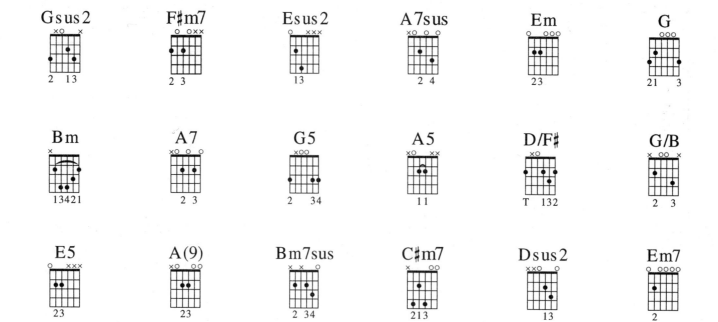

TO FORGIVE

Tune down 1/2 step:
⑥ = E♭ ③ = G♭
⑤ = A♭ ② = B♭
④ = D♭ ① = E♭

Words and Music by
BILLY CORGAN

Slow rock ♩ = 63

Intro:

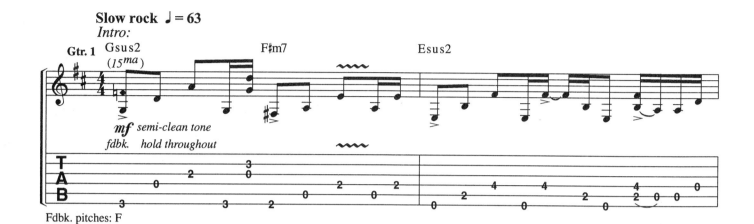

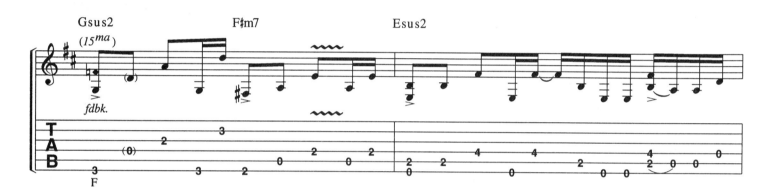

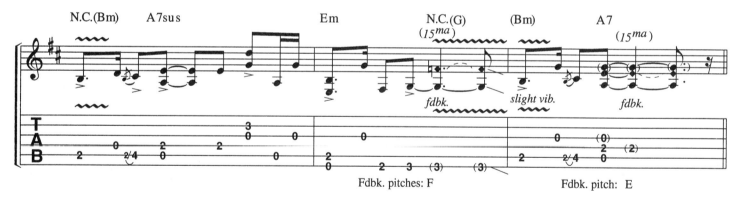

Verse 1:

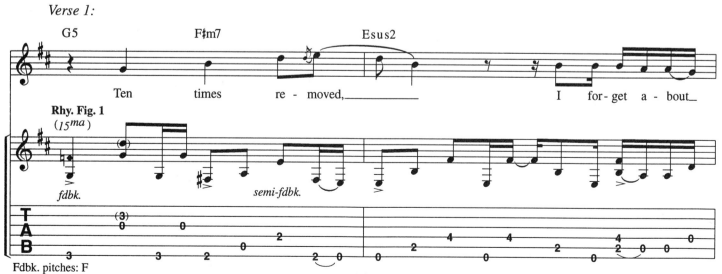

Fdbk. pitch: E

Chorus:

* Last time, "doubled" by 2nd gtr., w/wah (very low in mix).

To Coda II

To Coda I

Fdbk. pitch: E

ZERO

This song begins with octave shapes sliding from "C" to "B" (see frames below). The rest of the intro guitar figure is based on natural harmonics. The "B" and "G#" harmonics found at the 3rd and 4th frets aren't too hard to produce, just lightly touch the ⑥ string directly over the indicated fret, remove your finger from the string as soon as you sound the harmonic. The "D" harmonic is found somewhere in-between the 2nd and 3rd frets. Experiment until you find just the right spot on your guitar.

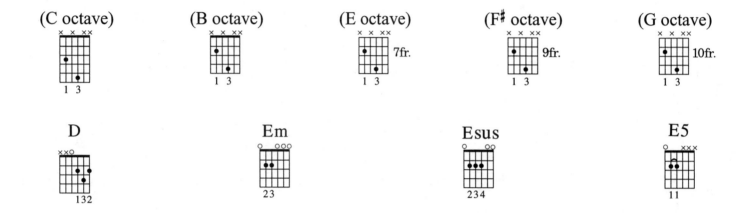

ZERO

Words and Music by
BILLY CORGAN

Tune down 1/2 step:
⑥ = E♭   ③ = G♭
⑤ = A♭   ② = B♭
④ = D♭   ① = E♭

Moderate rock ♩ =126
Intro:

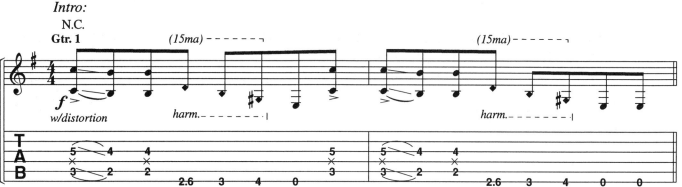

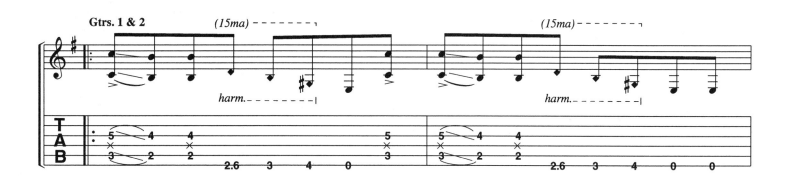

*Gtr. 1 tabbed on left;
Gtr. 2 tabbed on right.*

Verses 1 & 2:

1. My re - flec - tion,   dirt - y mir - ror,
2. *See additional lyrics*

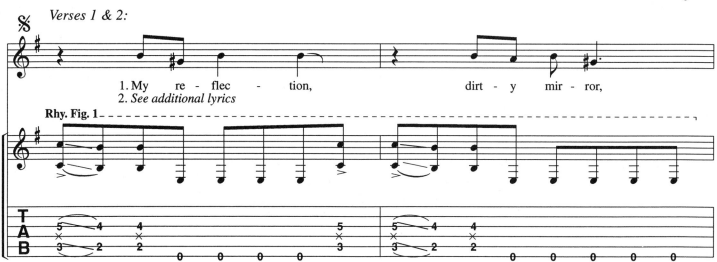

68

*Harmonizer produces atonal, high-pitched noises.

** All notes sound one octave higher due to harmonizer effect.

*Notes sound two octaves higher due to whammy pedal.

*This note sounds two octaves higher due to whammy pedal.

Zero - 8 - 7
PG9602

72

*All notes sound two octaves higher due to whammy pedal.

Verse 2:
Intoxicated with the madness, I'm in love with my sadness.
Bullshit fakers, enchanted kingdoms,
The fashion victims chew their charcoal teeth.

Pre-Chorus:
I never let on that I was a sinking ship.
I never let on that I was down.

Zero - 8 - 8
PG9602

FUCK YOU (AN ODE TO NO ONE)

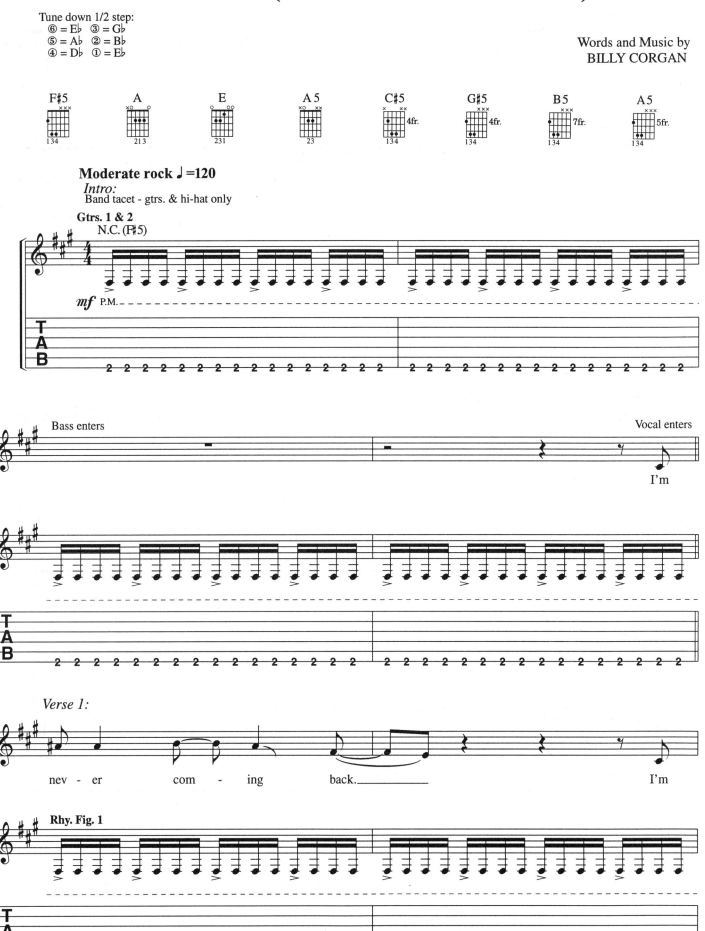

Words and Music by
BILLY CORGAN

Fuck You (An Ode To No One) - 16 - 1
PG9602

74

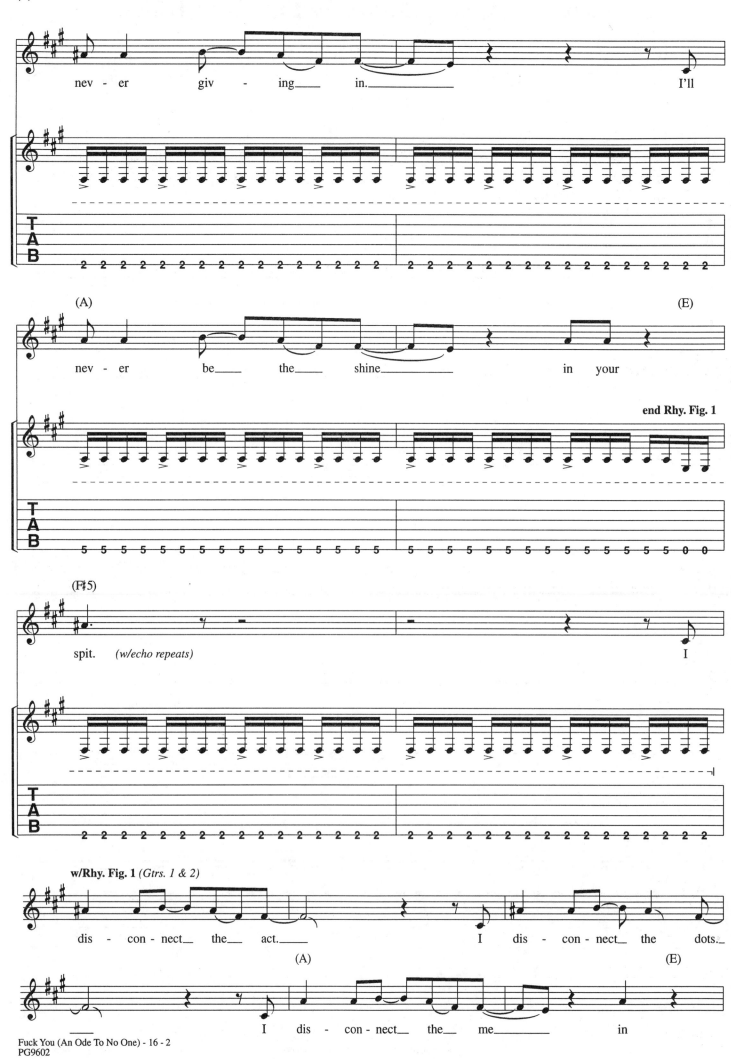

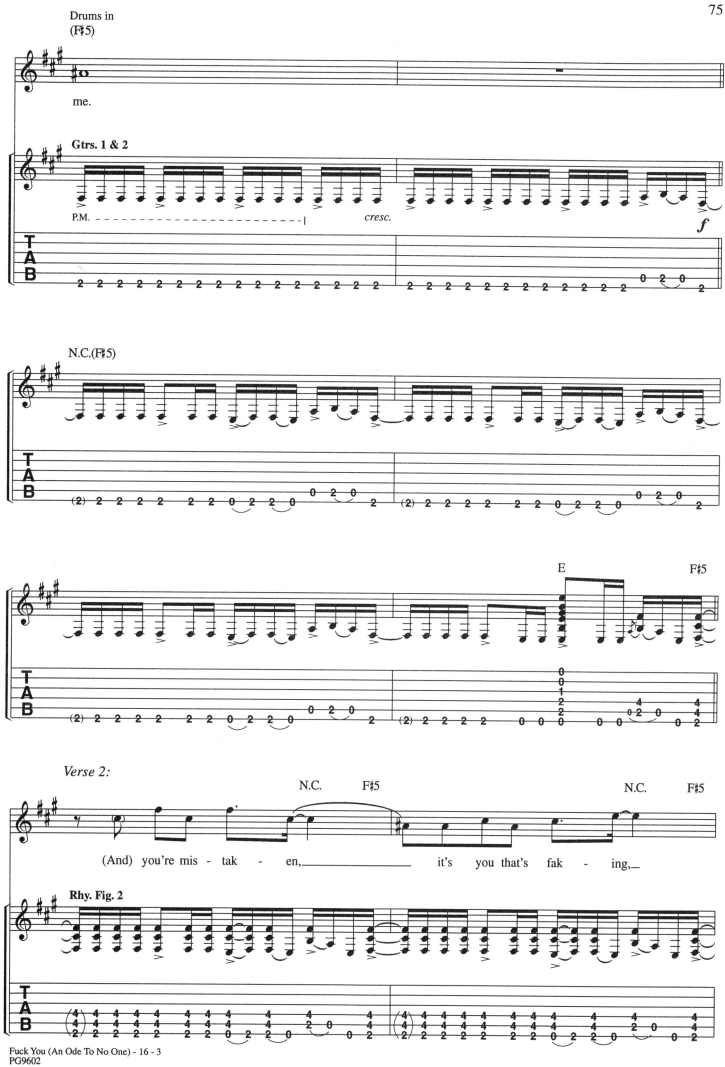

76

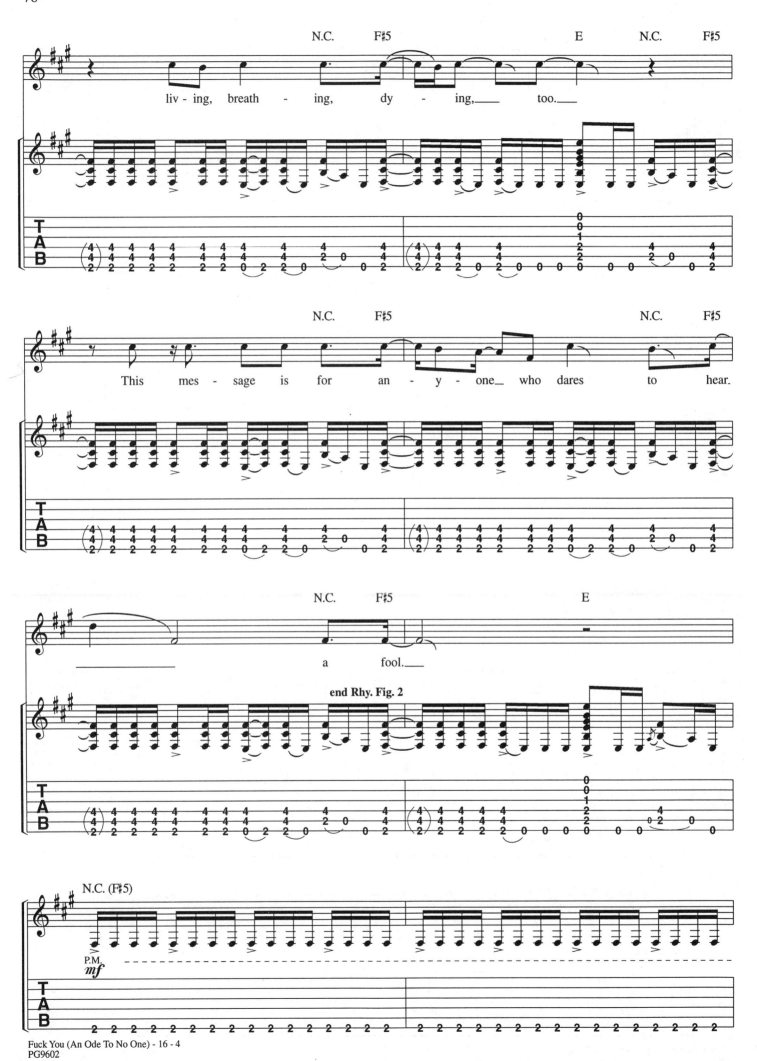

Fuck You (An Ode To No One) - 16 - 4
PG9602

78

Fuck You (An Ode To No One) - 16 - 8
PG9602

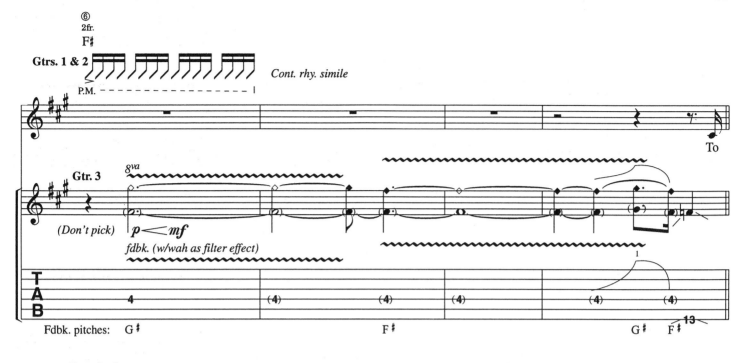

Fdbk. pitches: G♯   F♯   G♯ F♯

Interlude:

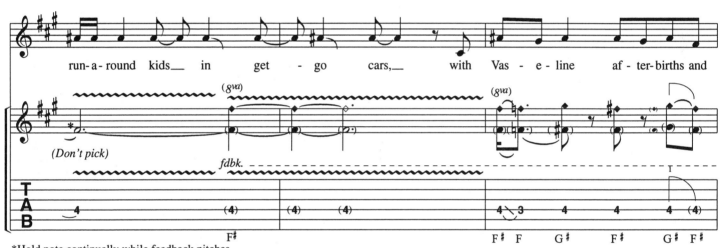

run-a-round kids___ in get-go cars,___ with Vas-e-line af-ter-births and

F♯   F♯ F   G♯   F♯   G♯ F♯

*Hold note continually while feedback pitches
change (guitar is held in different positions in
relation to amp, with none of the notes picked.)
Feedback occurs as the result of high volume and distortion.

ne-on coughs.___ Gal-ax-ies___ full of no-bod-ies,___

F♯ G   F♯   C♯   G♯ C   C♯   A♯

*Bend B (3rd stg./4th fr.) w/ 3rd finger, catching F♯ (4th stg./4th fr.) under it,
which subsequently produces next feedback note, A♯.

82

Fuck You (An Ode To No One) - 16 - 10
PG9602

Chorus 2:
w/Rhy. Fig. 3 *(Gtrs. 1 & 2)*

No— way, I don't need it, I don't need your— love_____ to dis - con - nect._

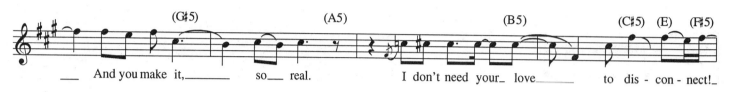

__ And you make it,_____ so__ real. I don't need your_ love_____ to dis - con - nect!_

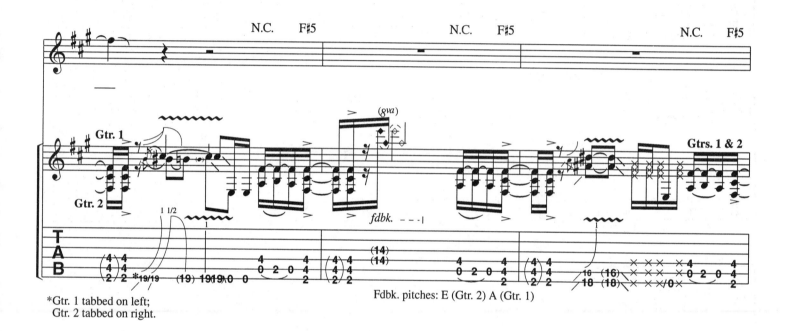

*Gtr. 1 tabbed on left;
Gtr. 2 tabbed on right.

Fdbk. pitches: E (Gtr. 2) A (Gtr. 1)

Guitar Solo:

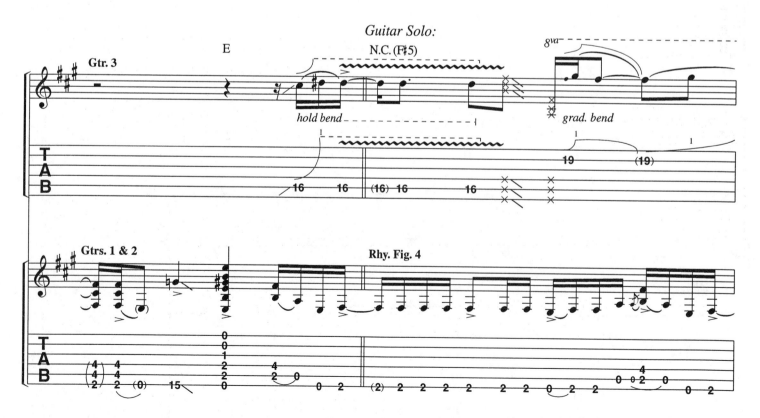

hold bend - - - - - - - - - - -|

grad. bend

Rhy. Fig. 4

Fuck You (An Ode To No One) - 16 - 14
PG9602

w/Rhy. Fig. 3 *(Gtrs. 1 & 2) bars 5-8 only*

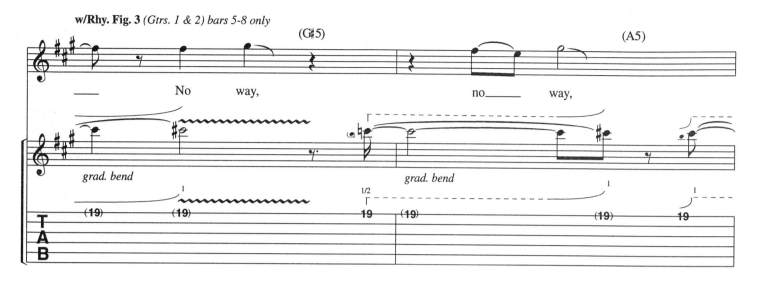

*Bend an additional quarter tone.

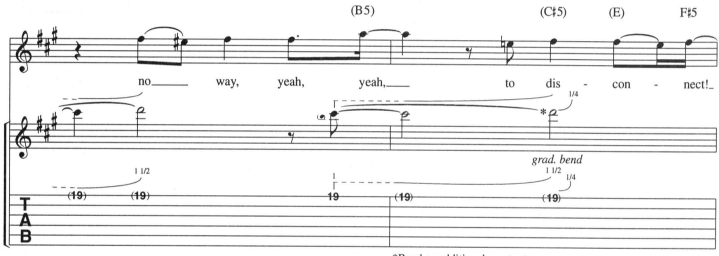

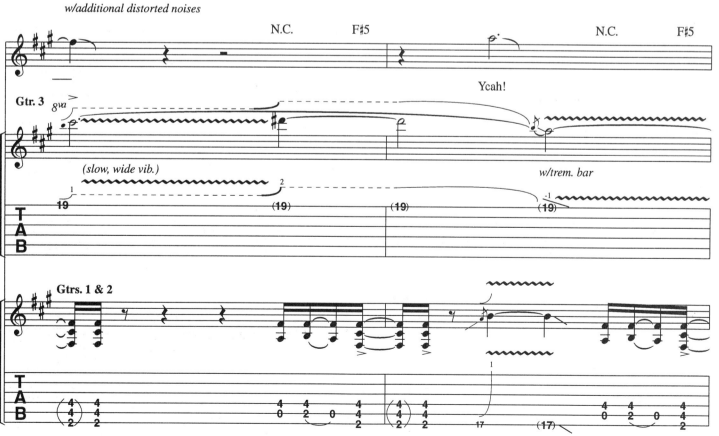

88

N.C.

F#5

Free time

E

w/Miscellaneous fdbk. (harmonic & microphonic)

w/trem. bar

*Begin bending neck.

(15ma)

fdbk.

w/trem. bar

Fdbk. pitch: D

LOVE

Tune down 1/2 step:
⑥ = E♭ ③ = G♭
⑤ = A♭ ②= B♭
④ = D♭ ① = E♭

Words and Music by
BILLY CORGAN

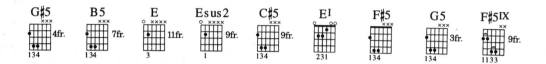

Moderate rock ♩ = 96
Intro:
Band tacet

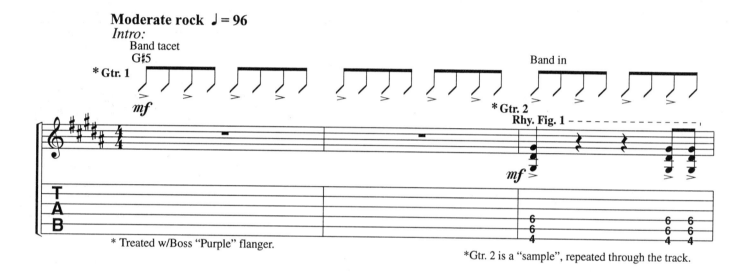

* Treated w/Boss "Purple" flanger.

*Gtr. 2 is a "sample", repeated through the track.

Verses 1 & 2:
w/Rhy. Fig. 1 *(Gtr. 2) 4 times*

1. To my mis - takes,_____   to my mis - takes___ of__ cow - ard - ice.
2. *See additional lyrics*

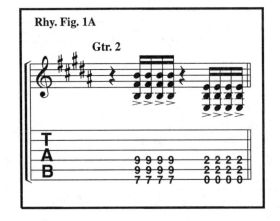

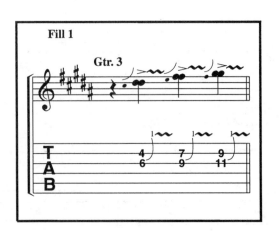

Bridge:

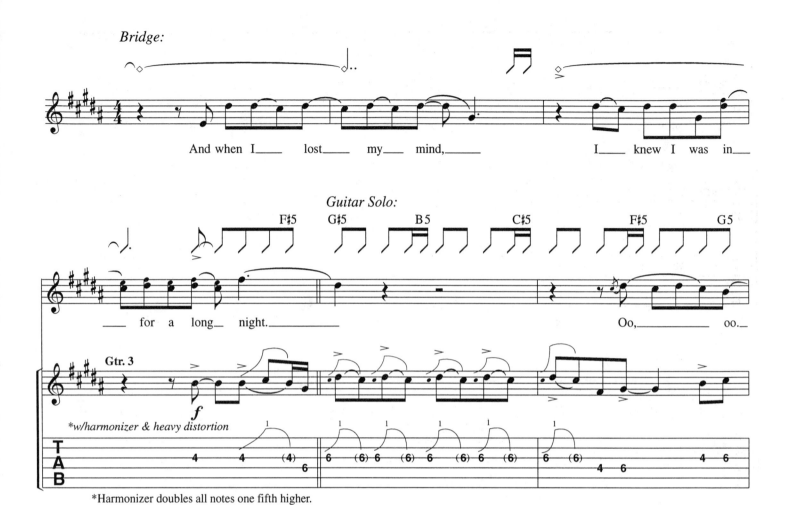

And when I___ lost___ my___ mind,___ I___ knew I was in___

Guitar Solo:

___ for a long___ night.____ Oo,_____ oo.__

Gtr. 3

w/harmonizer & heavy distortion

*Harmonizer doubles all notes one fifth higher.

Ah, oo,___ ha hoo. Ah.___ Hmm,

grad. bend

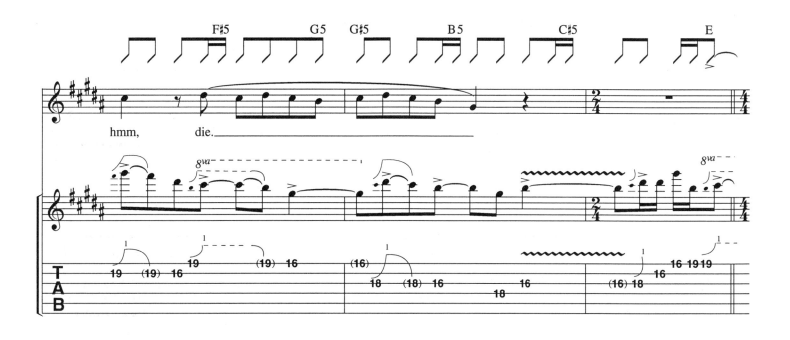

Pre-Chorus 2:

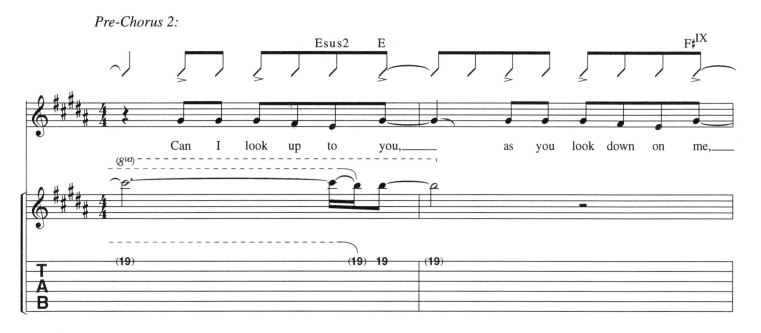

Can I look up to you,_____ as you look down on me,_____

_____ can I feel in-to you,_____ as you felt in-to me?_____ I can't help what you see,

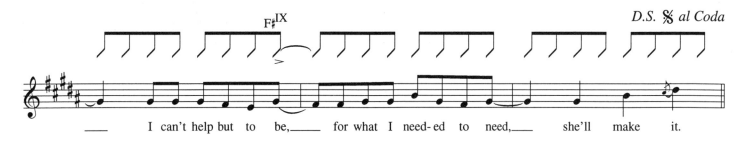

_____ I can't help but to be,_____ for what I need-ed to need,_____ she'll make it.

Love - 6 - 5
PG9602

94

Verse 2:
Machine gun blues, her vacant rush is so steel.
I'm unaware, lost inside your visions.
I got mine too over, I got mine and I got you.
'Cause I know you, you're love.

CUPID DE LOCKE

Tune down 1/2 step:
⑥ = E♭ ③ = G♭
⑤ = A♭ ② = B♭
④ = D♭ ① = E♭

Words and Music by
BILLY CORGAN

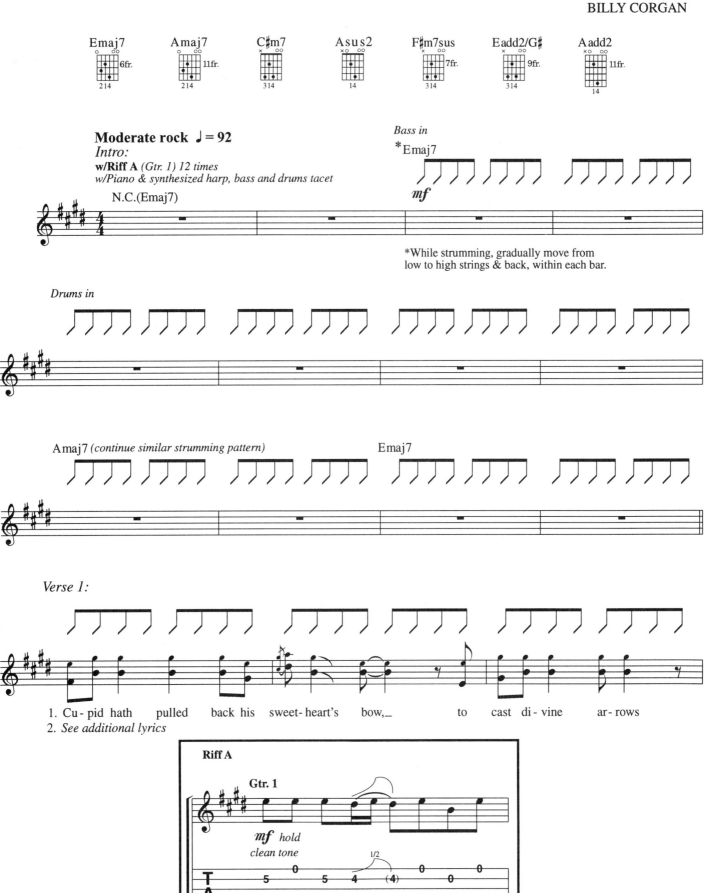

Moderate rock ♩ = 92
Intro:
w/Riff A *(Gtr. 1) 12 times*
w/Piano & synthesized harp, bass and drums tacet

Bass in
*Emaj7

*While strumming, gradually move from
low to high strings & back, within each bar.

Drums in

Amaj7 *(continue similar strumming pattern)*   Emaj7

Verse 1:

1. Cu-pid hath   pulled   back his   sweet-heart's   bow,__   to   cast di-vine   ar-rows
2. *See additional lyrics*

Riff A

Gtr. 1

mf hold
clean tone

one Cu - pid's ar - row un - der your__ coat.

Outro:
w/recitation (see below)

Sing,__ yeah,__ yeah,__ yeah._____

Sing,__ yeah,__ yeah,__ yeah._____ Sing,__ yeah,__ yeah,__ yeah. Sing,__ yeah,__ yeah,__ yeah.

Sing,__ yeah,__ yeah,__ yeah. Sing,__ yeah,__ yeah,__ yeah._____

Recitation:
And in the land of star-crossed lovers,
And barren-hearted wanderers,
Forever lost in forsaken missives and Satan's pull,
We seek the unseekable and we speak the unspeakable,
Our hopes dead, gathering dust to dust
In faith, in compassion and in love.

Verse 2:
See, the devil may do as the devil may care.
He loves none sweeter than sweeter the dare.
Her mouth the mischief he doth seek.
Her heart the captive of which he speaks.

Chorus 2:
So note all ye lovers in love with the sound.
Your world be shattered with nary a note
Of one cupid's arrow under your coat.

GALAPOGOS

D(2)

Dmaj7

Em/D

Bm7

D/F#

Em

G

D(9)

Em7/D

D5

F#m sus

Em(9)

Dsus2

A

Gm/B♭

C

Em7

GALAPOGOS

Words and Music by
BILLY CORGAN

Tune down 1/2 step:
⑥ = E♭ ③ = G♭
⑤ = A♭ ② = B♭
④ = D♭ ① = E♭

Slow rock ♩ = 58

Intro:

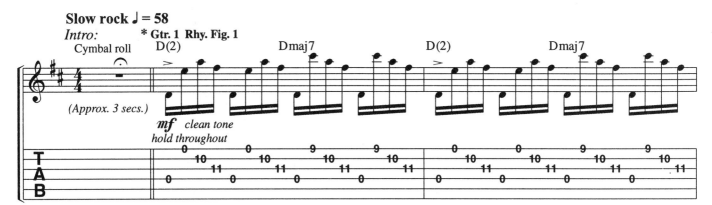

*Doubled by another gtr.

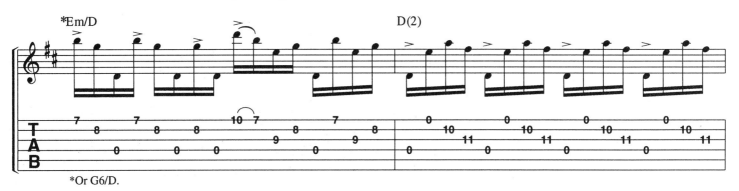

*Or G6/D.

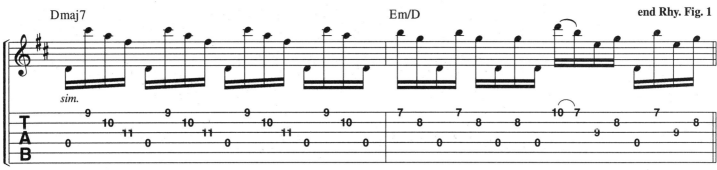

Verse 1:
w/Rhy. Fig. 1 *(Gtr. 1)*

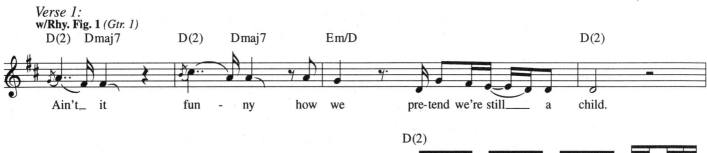

Ain't__ it fun - ny how we pre-tend we're still__ a child.

Soft - ly sto - len un-der__ our blan - ket skies.

100

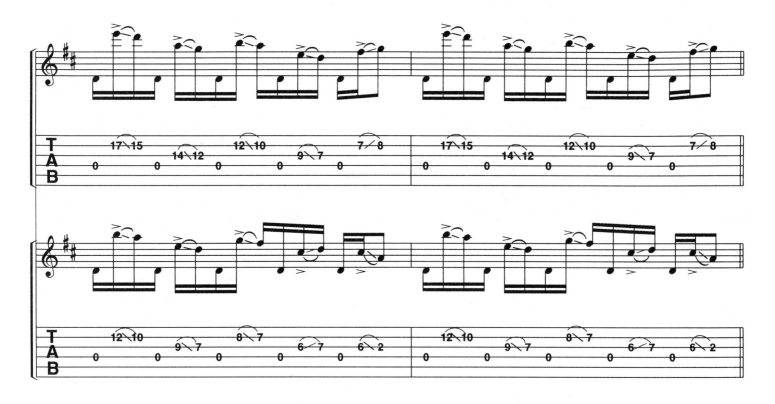

Interlude:

Gtrs. 1 & 2

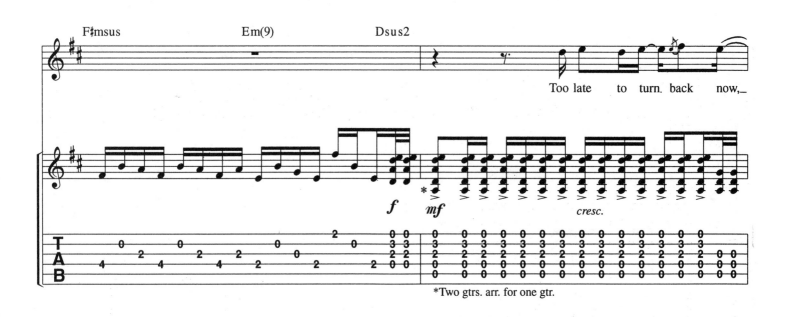

Too late   to   turn. back   now,_

*Two gtrs. arr. for one gtr.

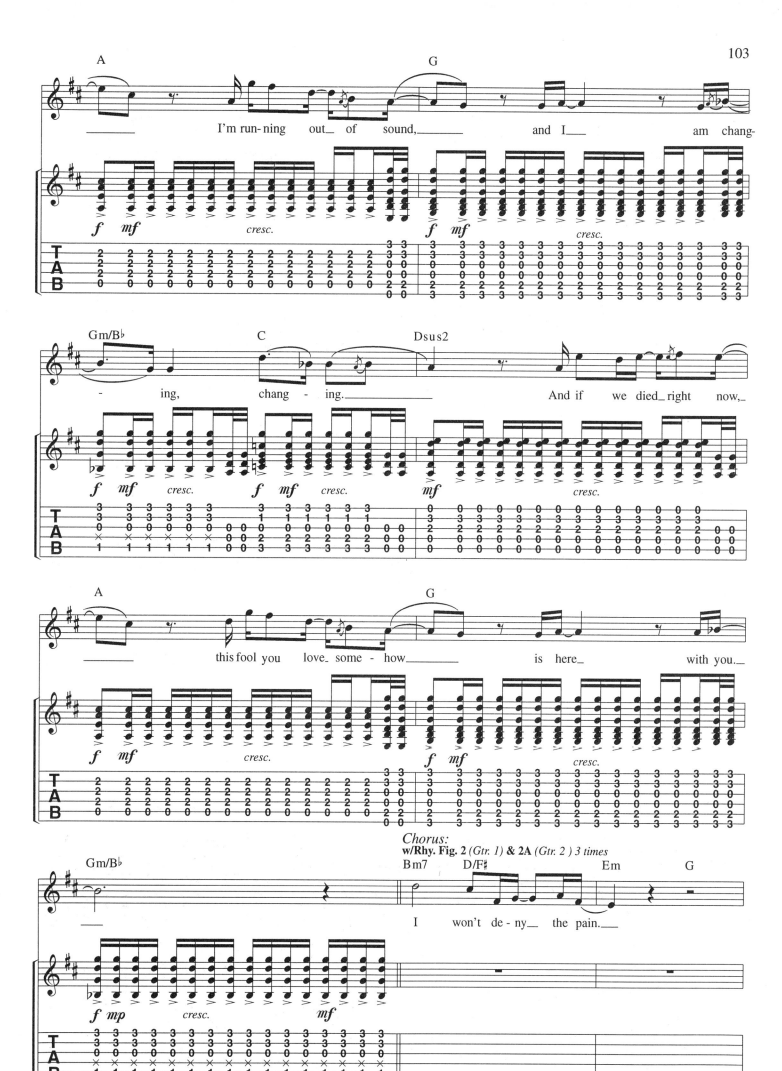

MUZZLE

Words and Music by
BILLY CORGAN

*Tune down 1/2 step:
⑥ = E♭   ③ = G♭
⑤ = A♭   ② = A♭
④ = D♭   ① = E♭

A5   G(9)   Bm7(11)   Dsus2   B7sus   E

*This song uses an altered tuning, the "B" (②) string is tuned down a whole-step to "A". Billy then uses simple chord shapes in combination with the ringing open ① and ② strings (E and A) to produce some beautiful chord sounds.

Moderate rock ♩ = 88

*Gtr. 2 is a Les Paul, with a thicker, much more distorted tone. Gtr. 1 is a Stratocaster.

Muzzle - 8 - 1
PG9602

110

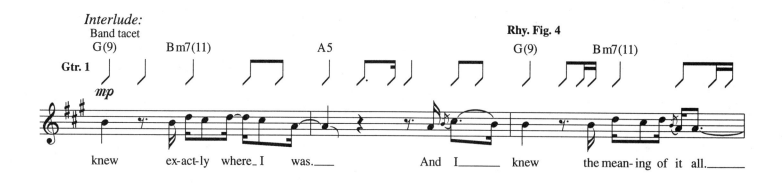

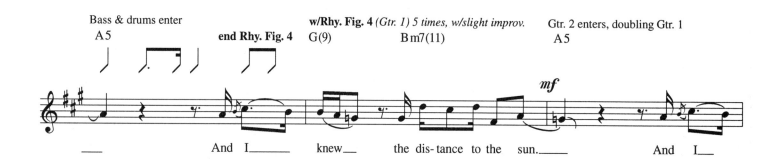

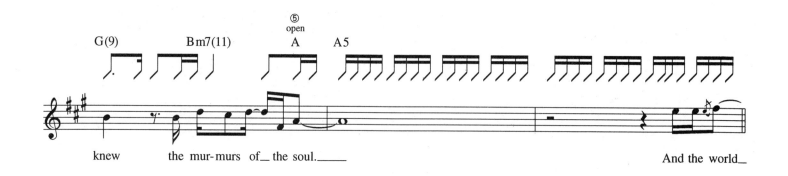

TAKE ME DOWN

Tune down 1/2 step:
⑥ = E♭ ③ = G♭
⑤ = A♭ ② = B♭
④ = D♭ ① = E♭

Words and Music by
JAMES IHA

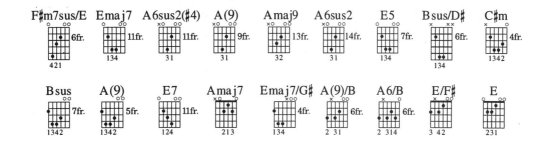

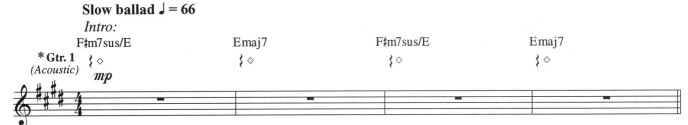

Slow ballad ♩ = 66

Intro:

*w/light chorusing & echo. (doubled by another acoustic gtr.)

Verse 1:

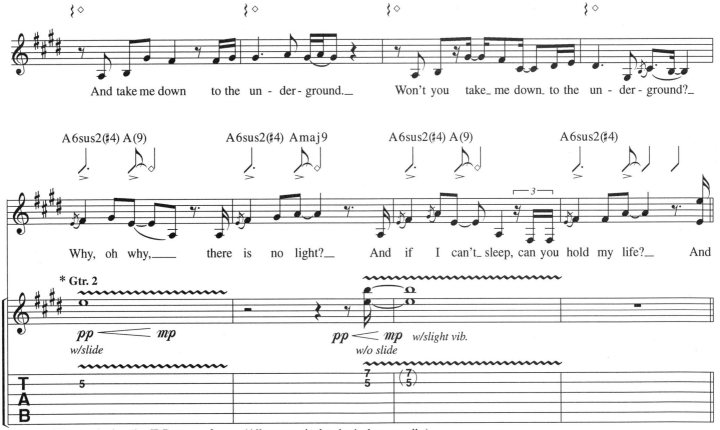

*Lap-steel, played w/E-Bow, arr. for gtr. (All notes articulated w/volume swells.)

114

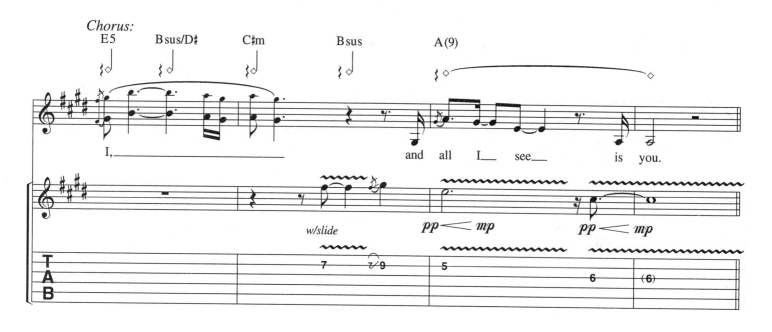

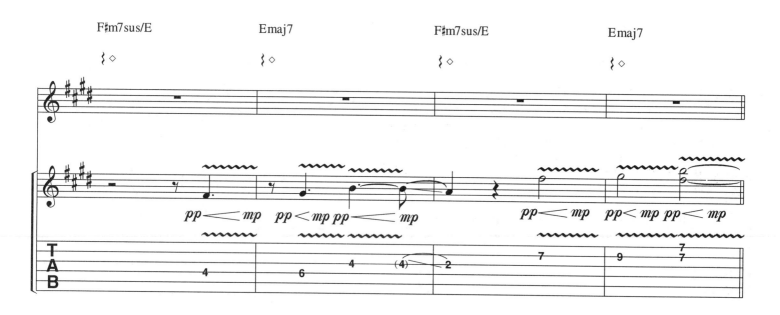

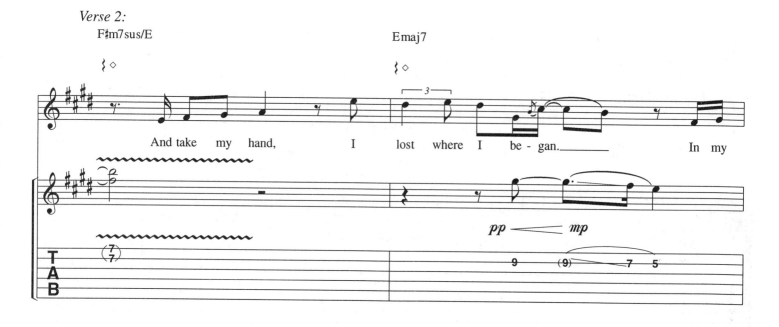

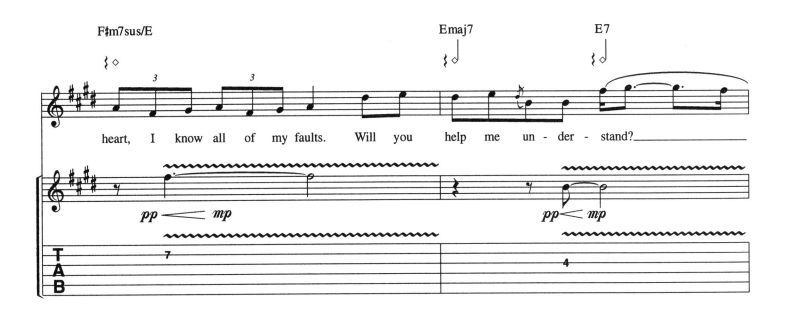

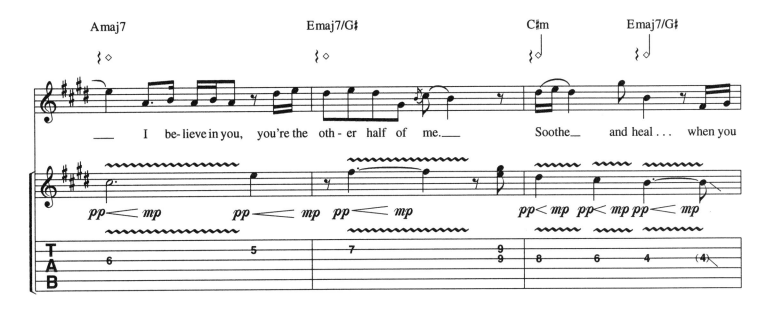

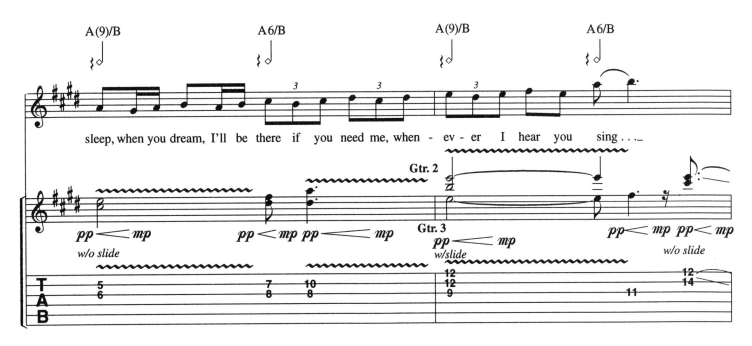

116

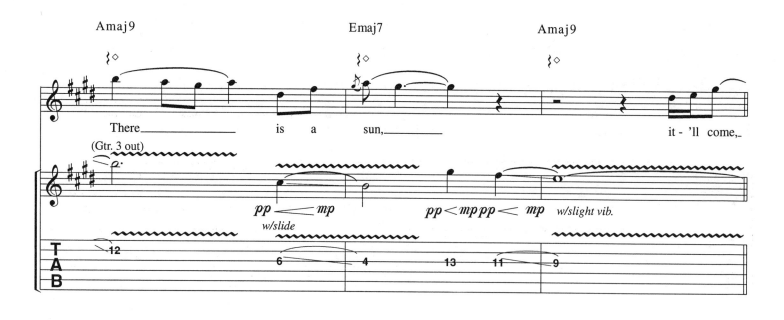

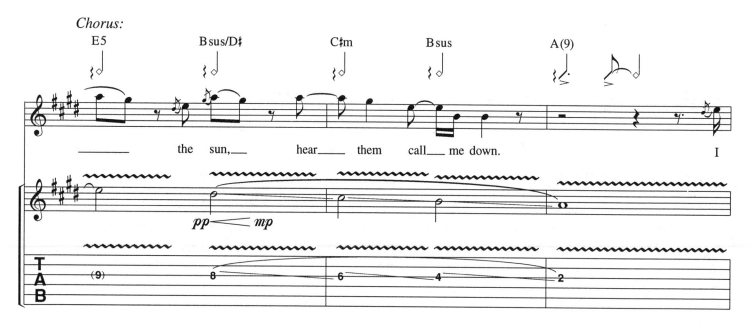

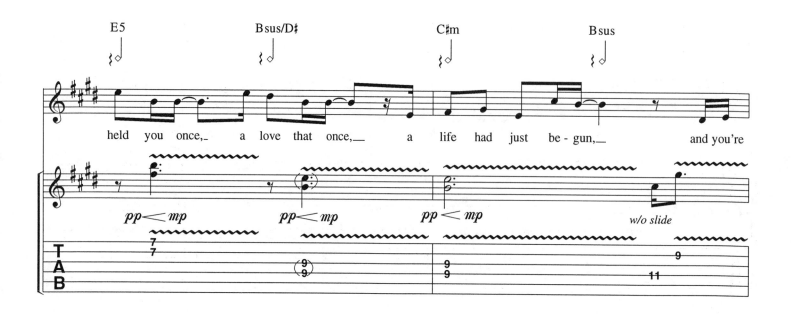

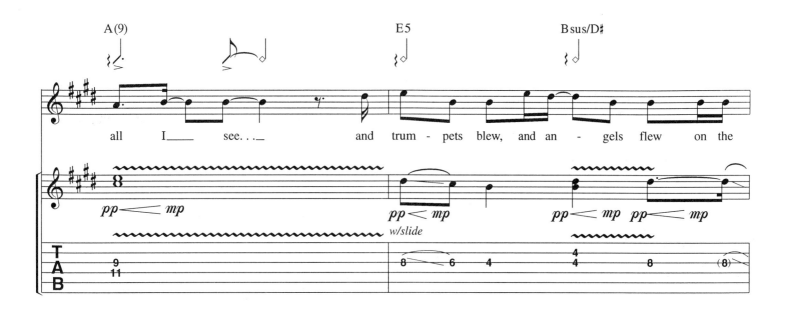

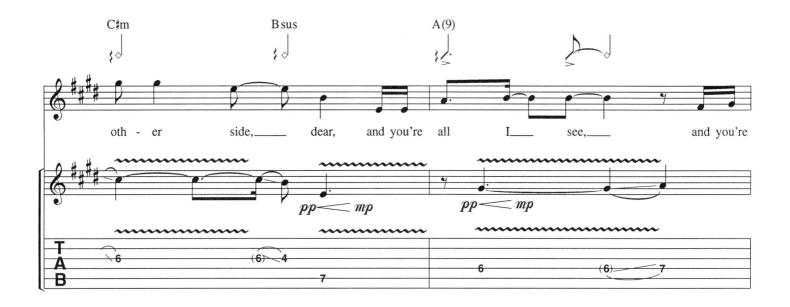

PORCELINA OF THE VAST OCEANS

A(2)

Am9

A

C($\frac{9}{b}$)

G5

Asus2

C(9)

D(2)

Csus2

C

G

D

A

C

G

PORCELINA OF THE VAST OCEANS

Words and Music by
BILLY CORGAN

Tune down 1/2 step:
⑥ = D♭ ③ = G♭
⑤ = A♭ ② = B♭
④ = D♭ ① = E♭

"Dropped D" tuning,
1/2 step low.

Slow rock ♩=48

Intro: w/miscellaneous fdbk. and overdubbed effects (through first 26 bars only)

*This figure steadily fades in very slowly; by the 6th time it's played, it has faded in fully to **mf**.

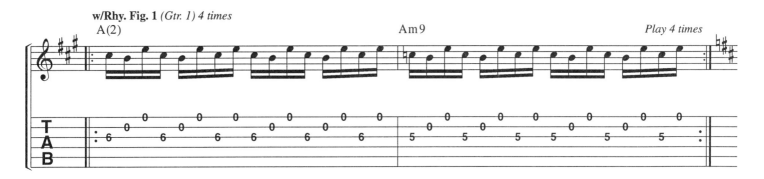

Double-time ♩ = 112

Porcelina Of The Vast Oceans - 16 - 1
PG9602

120

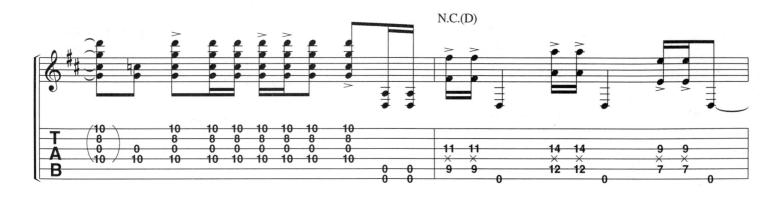

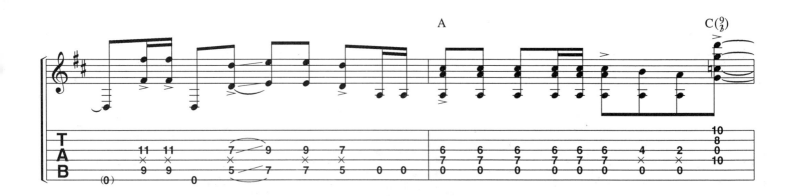

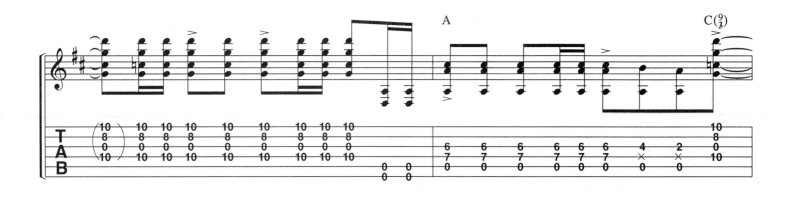

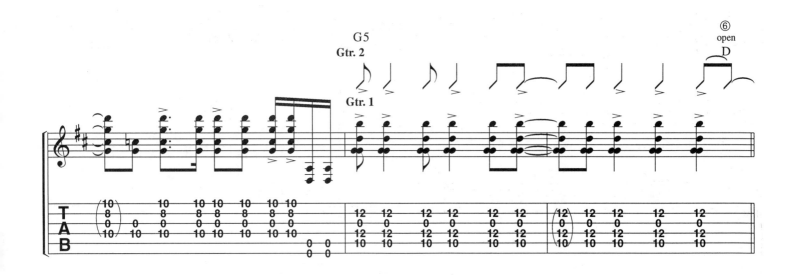

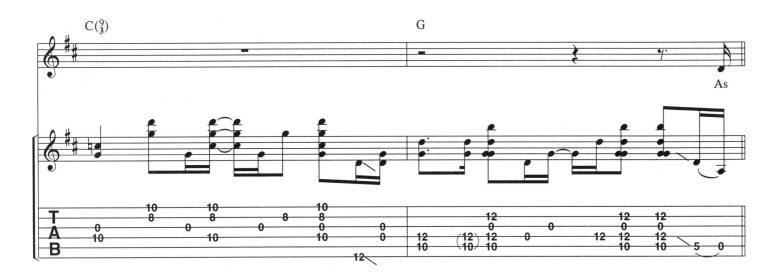

Verse 1:

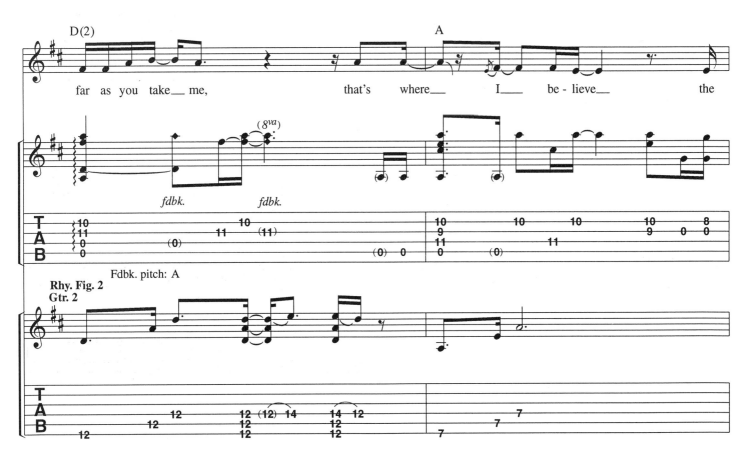

far as you take__ me, that's where__ I__ be - lieve__ the

122

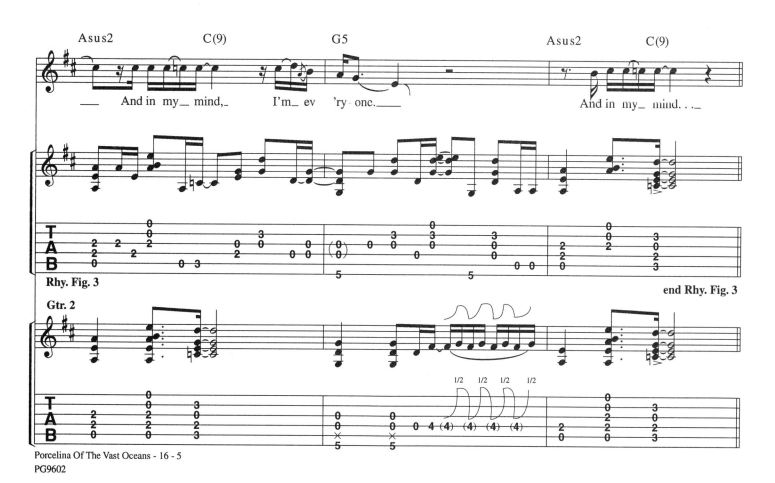

Porcelina Of The Vast Oceans - 16 - 5
PG9602

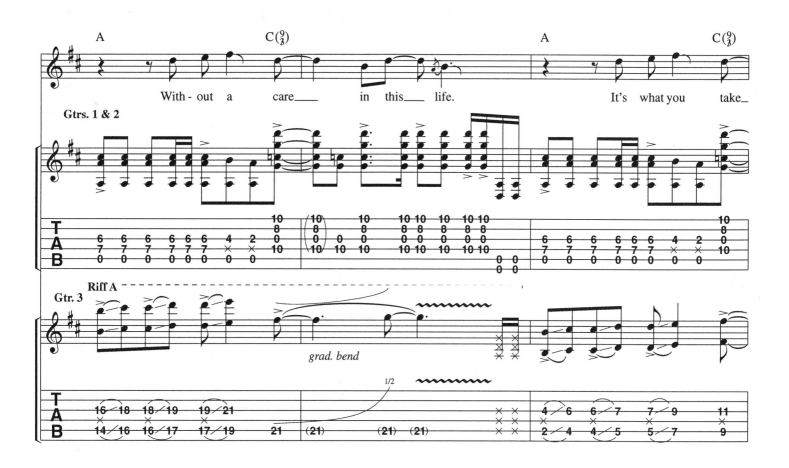

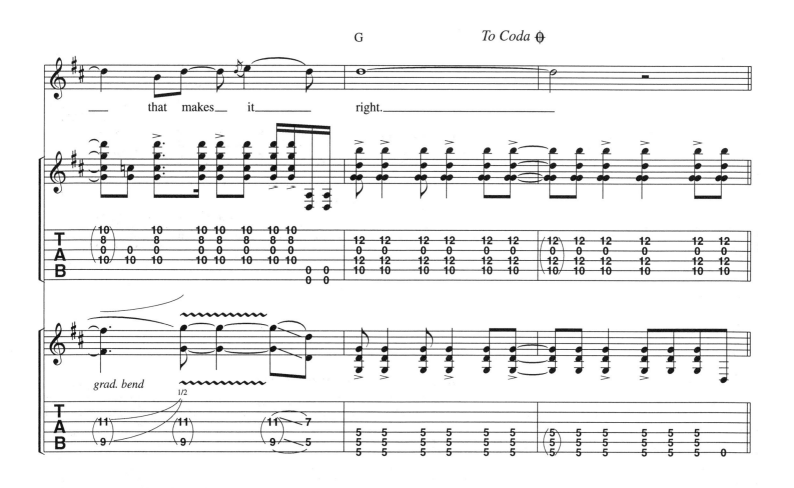

126

In time

Verse 2:

In the slip - stream___ of___ thought - less___ thoughts,__ the

Gtr. 1 tabbed on right;
Gtr. 3 tabbed on left.

Rhy. Fig. 4

light of all___ that's good,___ the light of all___ that's true.___ To the

Porcelina Of The Vast Oceans - 16 - 10
PG9602

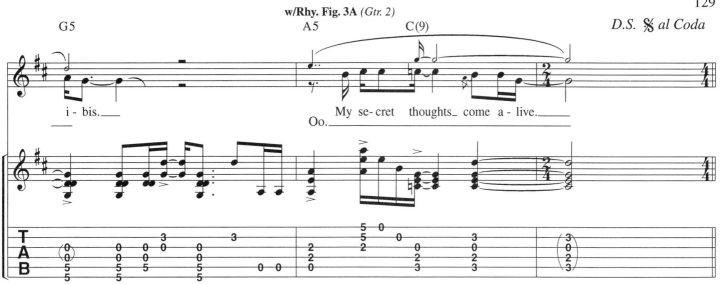

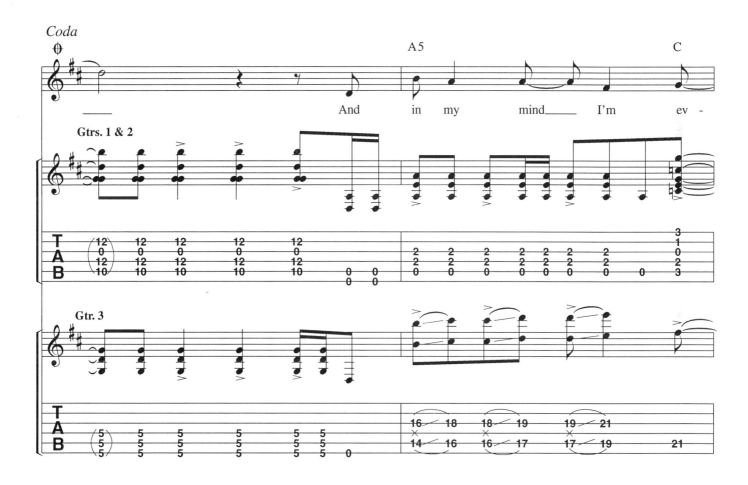

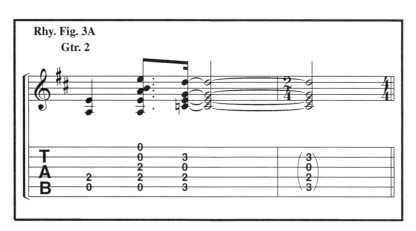

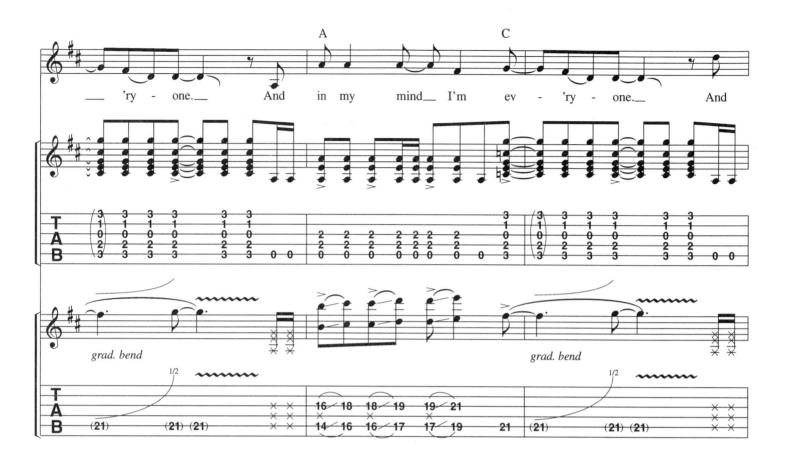

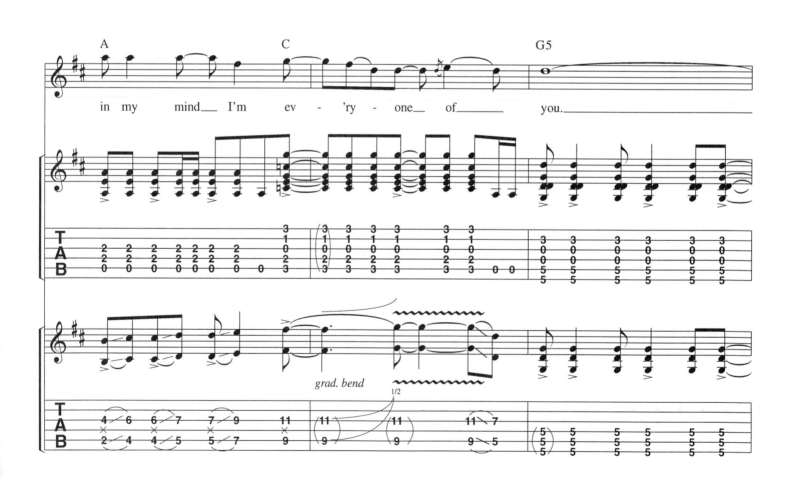

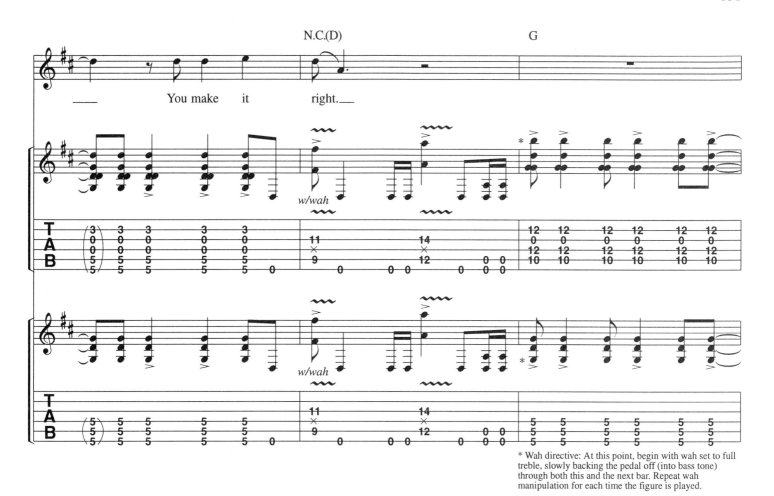

N.C.(D)　　　　　　　　　　　　　　　G

You make　it　right.___

w/wah

* Wah directive: At this point, begin with wah set to full
treble, slowly backing the pedal off (into bass tone)
through both this and the next bar. Repeat wah
manipulation for each time the figure is played.

N.C.(D)　　　　　　　　　　　　　　　G5

It's all al -　right.___

w/wah

Half-time ♩ = 54

Chorus 3: w/additional keybd. effects

*Gtr. 4

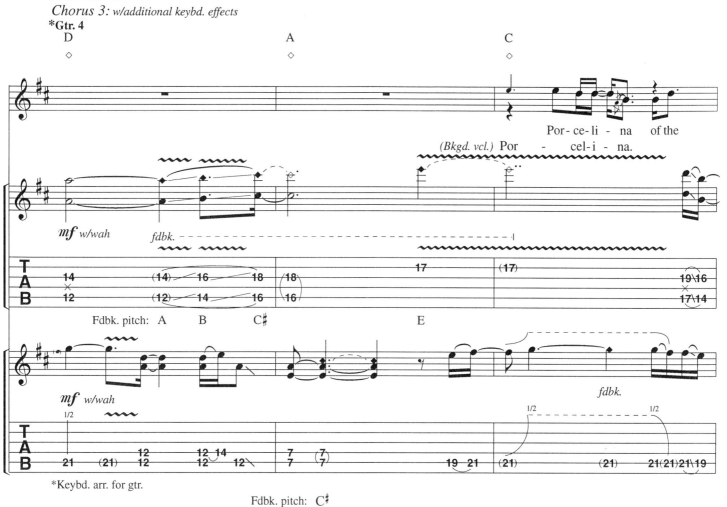

*Keybd. arr. for gtr.

Fdbk. pitch: C♯

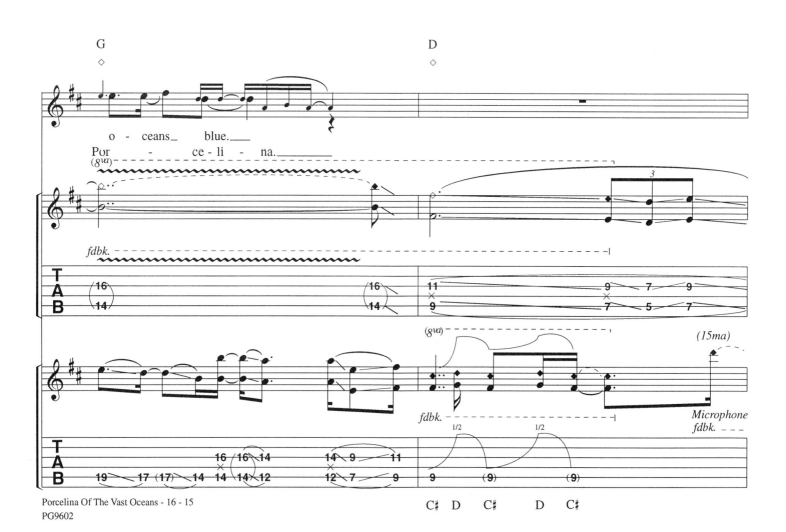

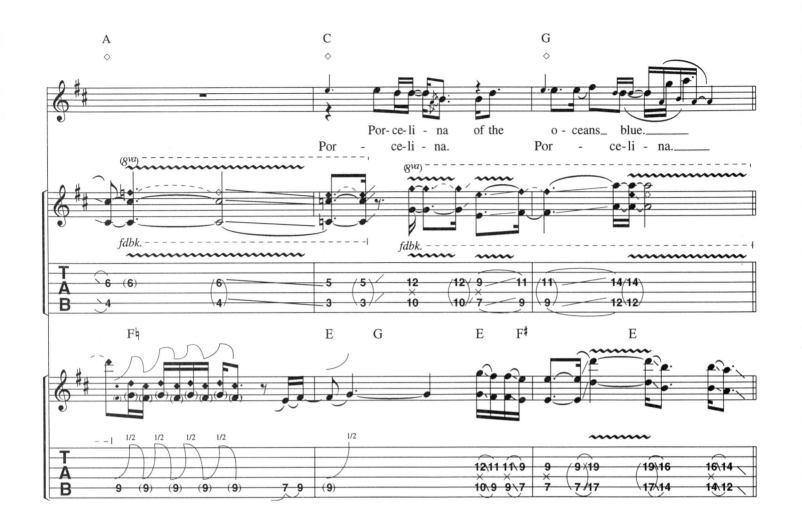

Por-ce-li - na of the o - ceans_ blue._____
Por - ce-li - na. Por - ce-li - na._____

Outro: *w/additional keybd. effects*

Repeat & continue ad lib.
feedback till fade

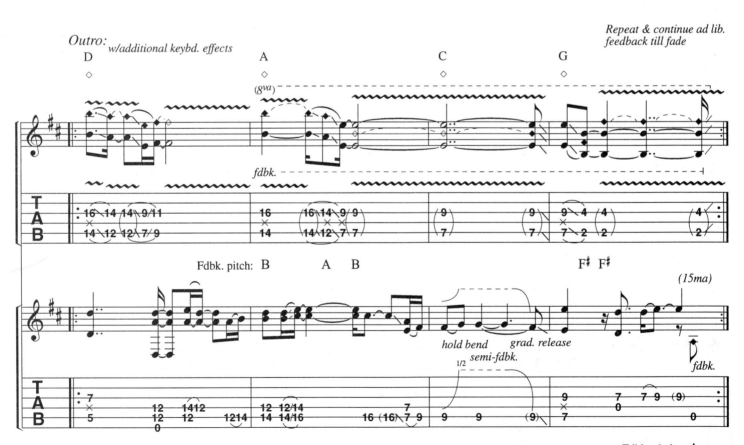

WHERE BOYS FEAR TO TREAD

Words and Music by
BILLY CORGAN

* String scrape.

136

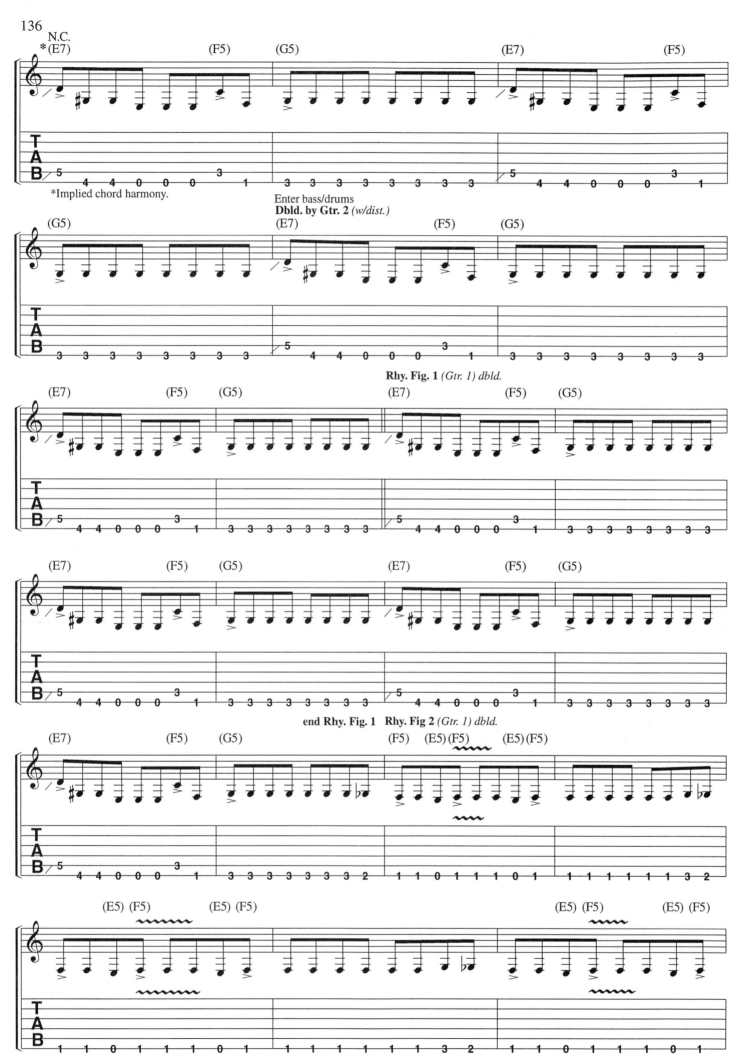

*Implied chord harmony.

Where Boys Fear To Tread - 5 - 2
PG9602

138

Where Boys Fear To Tread - 5 - 4
PG9602

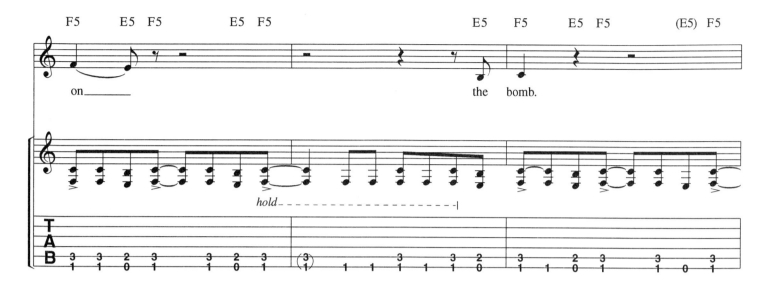

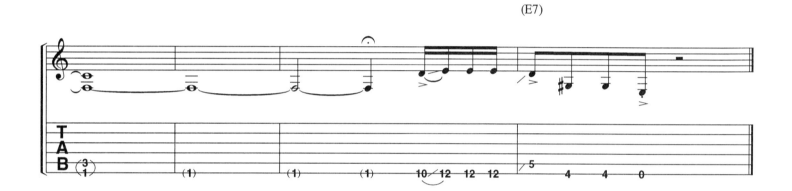

Verse 4:
On dead highways, her black beauties roam
For June angels so far from home.
For a love lost, a faded picture,
To tread lightning…

BODIES

Guitar 1 is tuned to "dropped D" — the ⑥ string is tuned down a whole-step to "D". This song is very "riff" based, the chord symbols in parentheses indicate the implied chords. The following chord frames show how the implied chords would be voiced in "dropped D" tuning. To match the recording, tune the whole guitar down one half-step.

G5

G♭5

F5

A5

D5

C(9)

F(9)

F

Am

C

Em

Dm

G5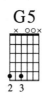

BODIES

Gtr. 1 tune down 1/2 step:
⑥ = D♭ ③ = G♭
⑤ = A♭ ② = B♭
④ = D♭ ① = E♭

"Dropped D" tuning,
1/2 step low.

Moderately fast ♩= 114

Words and Music by
BILLY CORGAN

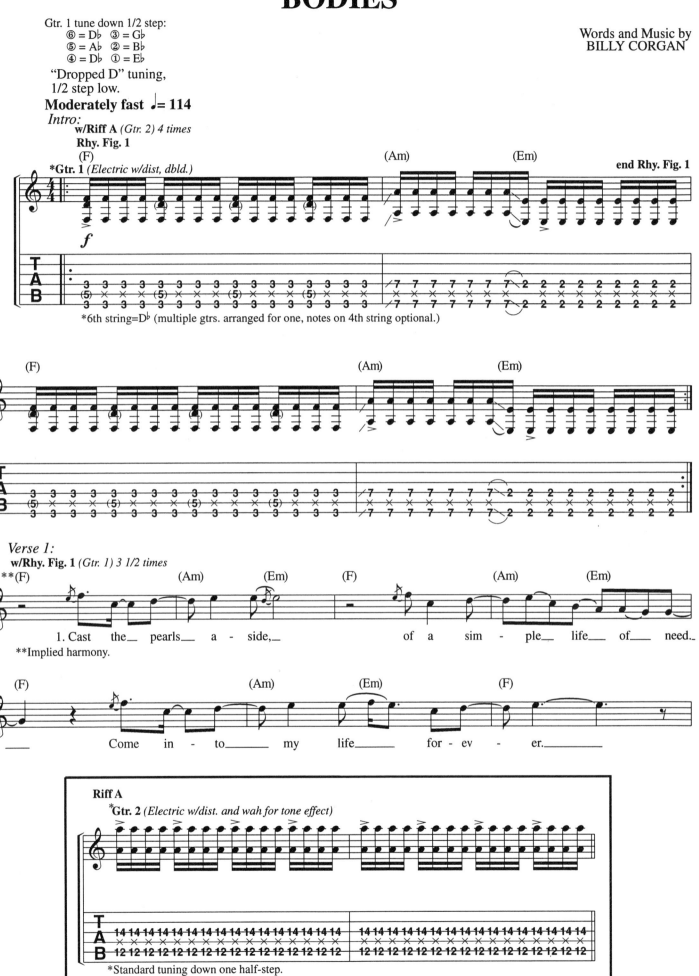

*6th string=D♭ (multiple gtrs. arranged for one, notes on 4th string optional.)

1. Cast the pearls aside, of a simple life of need.
**Implied harmony.

Come in-to my life for-ev-er.

Riff A
*Gtr. 2 (Electric w/dist. and wah for tone effect)

*Standard tuning down one half-step.

Bodies - 6 - 1
PG9602

142

Bodies - 6 - 2
PG9602

144

Outro Chorus:
w/Rhy. Fig. 1 *(Gtr. 1) 3 1/2 times*
w/Riff A *(Gtr. 2) 4 times*

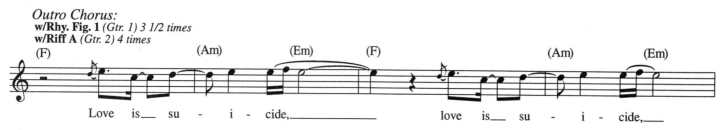

Love is su - i - cide,_____ love is su - i - cide,___

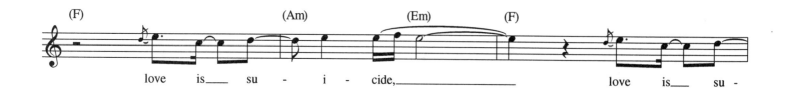

love is su - i - cide,_____ love is su -

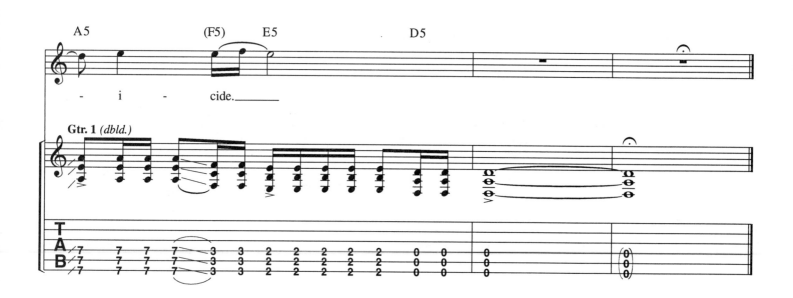

- i - cide._____

Verse 4:
All my blisters now revealed,
In the darkness of my dreams.
In the spaces in between us,
But no bodies ever...

THIRTY - THREE

All gtrs. tune down 1/2 step:
⑥ = E♭ ③ = G♭
⑤ = G♭ ② = B♭
④ = D♭ ① = E♭

Words and Music by
BILLY CORGAN

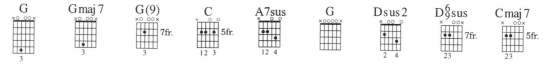

*The opening guitar figure is basically an open G chord with a shifting note on the ④ string. This shifting note forms the G, Gmaj7 and G(9) chord voicings shown in the first three frame diagrams.

Slow in 2 ♩ = 64

Intro:
Rhy. Fig. 1
  w/Riff A *(Gtr. 3)*

G

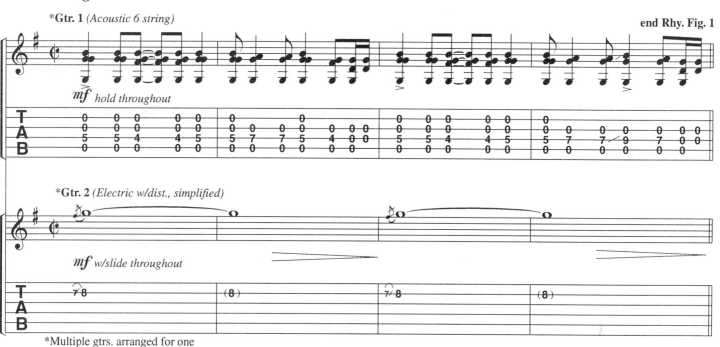

*Multiple gtrs. arranged for one

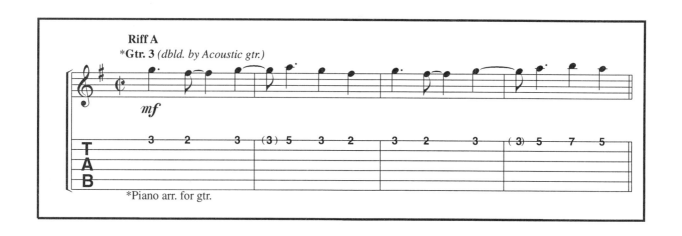

Verse:
w/Riff B (Gtr. 3)
G
C(9)
A7sus
1. Speak to me in a lan -
Rhy. Fig. 2
Lead Fig. 1
w/Rhy. Fig. 2 (Gtrs. 1 and 4) 7 times, simile
w/Riff B (Gtr. 3) 7 times, simile
G
- guage I can hear.
end Rhy. Fig. 2
end Lead Fig. 1
Riff B
*Gtr. 3 (dbld. by Acoustic gtr.)

150

Thirty-Three - 6 - 4

PG9602

152

can make it____ last for - ev - er,____ you____

can make it____ last for - ev - er,____ you,____

____ for - ev - er

Outro:
w/Rhy. Fig. 1 *(Gtr. 1) 1 1/2 times, simile*

you.

Gtr. 3 *(dbld. 8va)*

Verse 4:
I've journeyed here and there, and back again.
But in the same old haunts, I still find my friends.
Mysteries not ready to reveal.
Sympathies I'm ready to return.
I'll make the effort, love can last forever . . .

IN THE ARMS OF SLEEP

Gtrs. 1, 3 & 4 tune:
⑥ = E♭   ③ = G♮
⑤ = A♭   ② = B♭
④ = D♭   ① = E♭

Gtr. 2 standard tuning down 1/2 step.

Words and Music by
BILLY CORGAN

*Guitars 1, 3 and 4 use an interesting tuning on this song. Essentially, compared to standard tuning the ③ string is tuned up a half-step to G♯ (again the whole guitar is then tuned down a half-step to E♭). Billy then uses simple chord shapes in combination with the open strings to produce some really interesting chord sounds.

* See tuning guide.
** Multiple gtrs. w/ E-bow.
*** Gtrs. 3 and 4 are 12-string gtrs.
recorded at 1/2 speed,
written here for 6-string guitar.

154

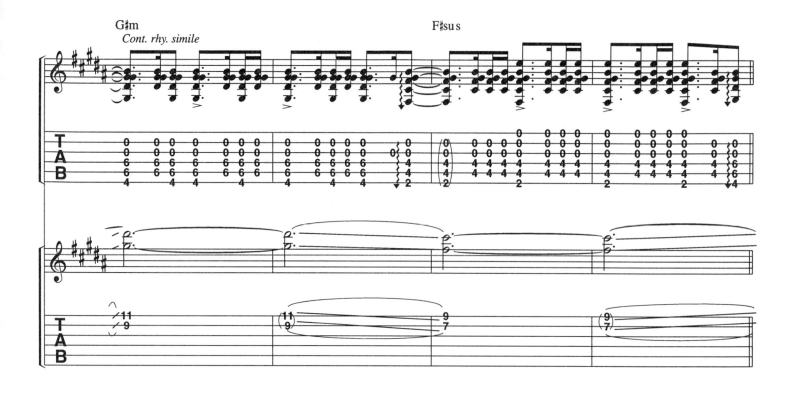

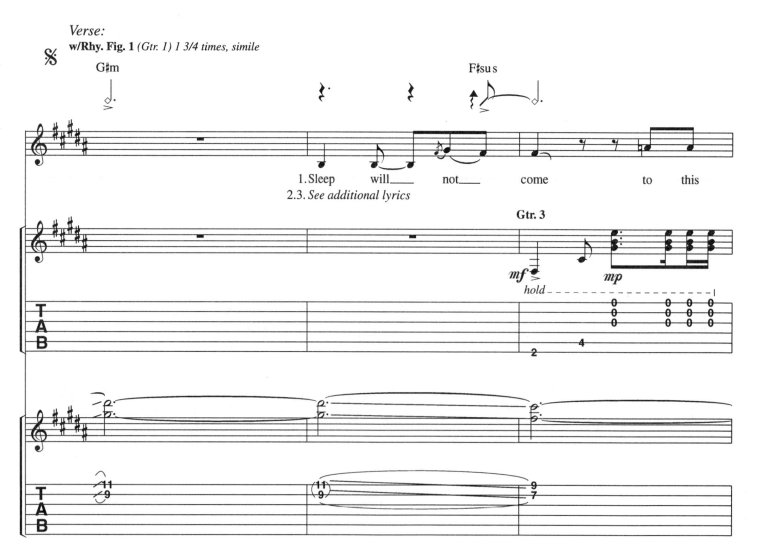

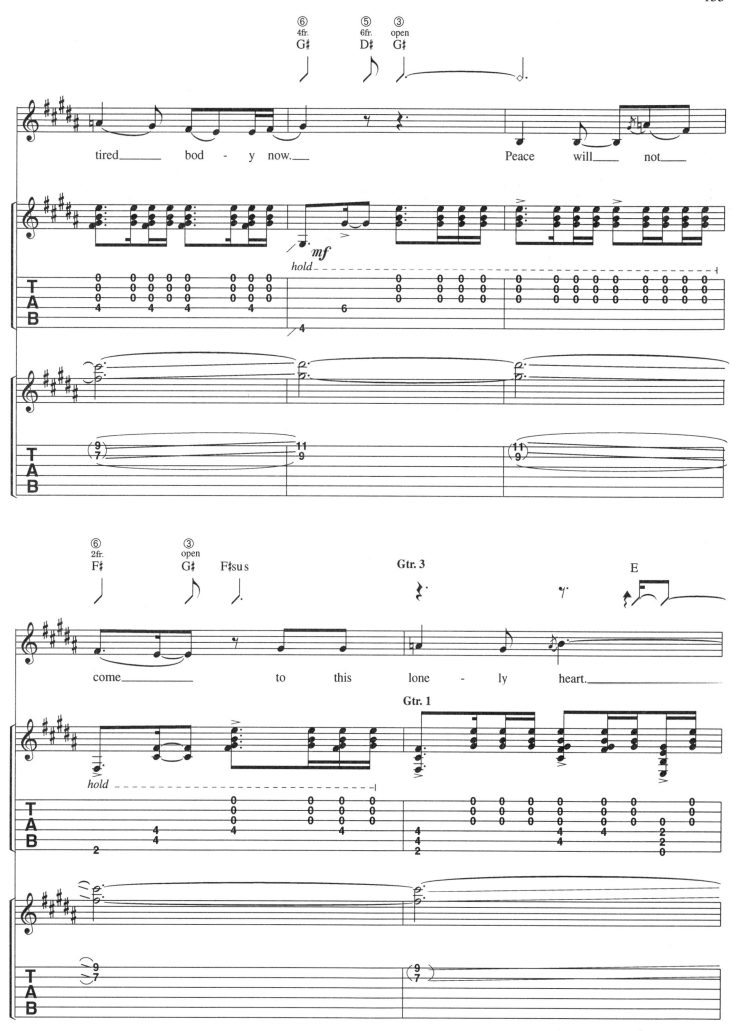

156

In The Arms Of Sleep - 11 - 4
PG9602

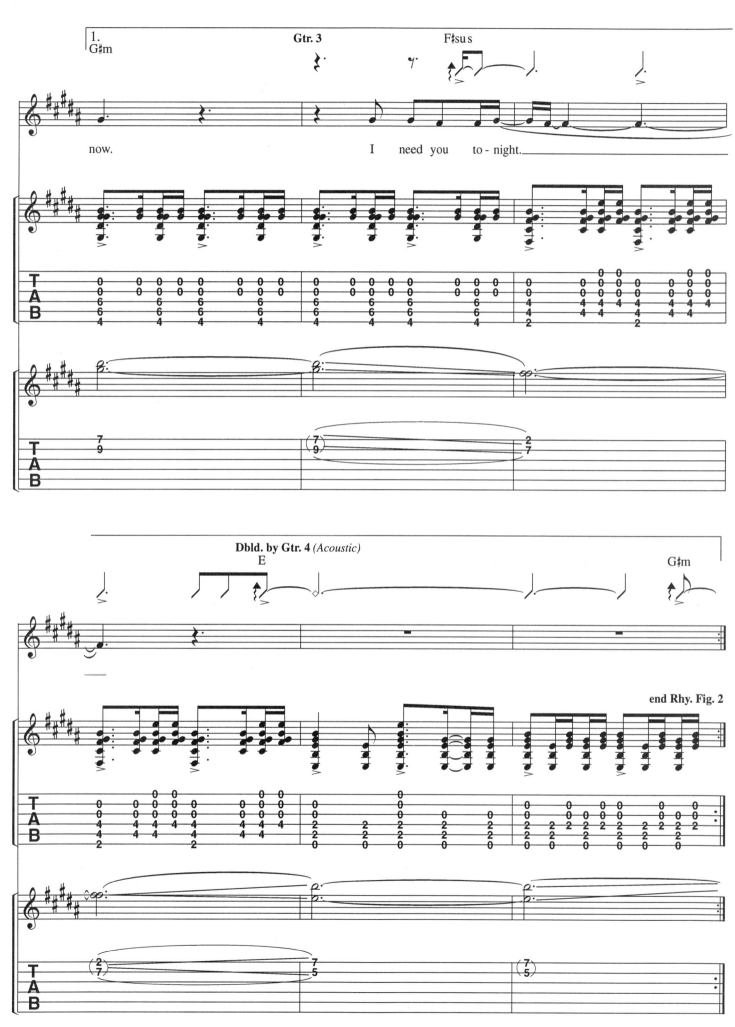

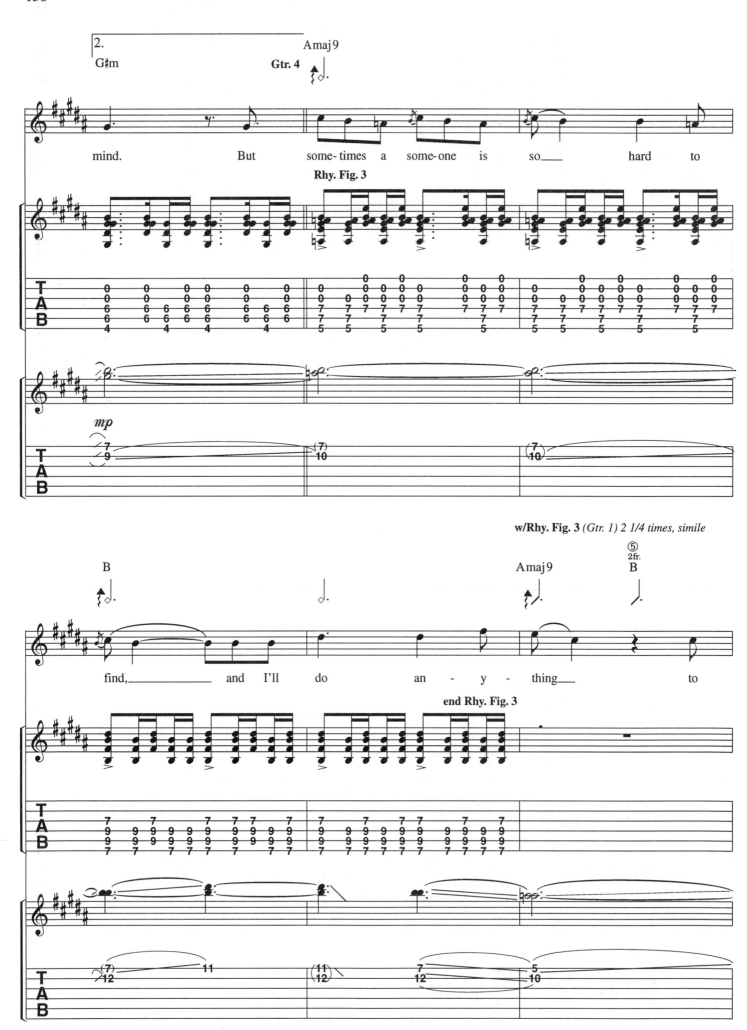

160

'Cause I want you to stay____ with me.____

I__ need you to-night.____

now.____

In The Arms Of Sleep - 11 - 8
PG9602

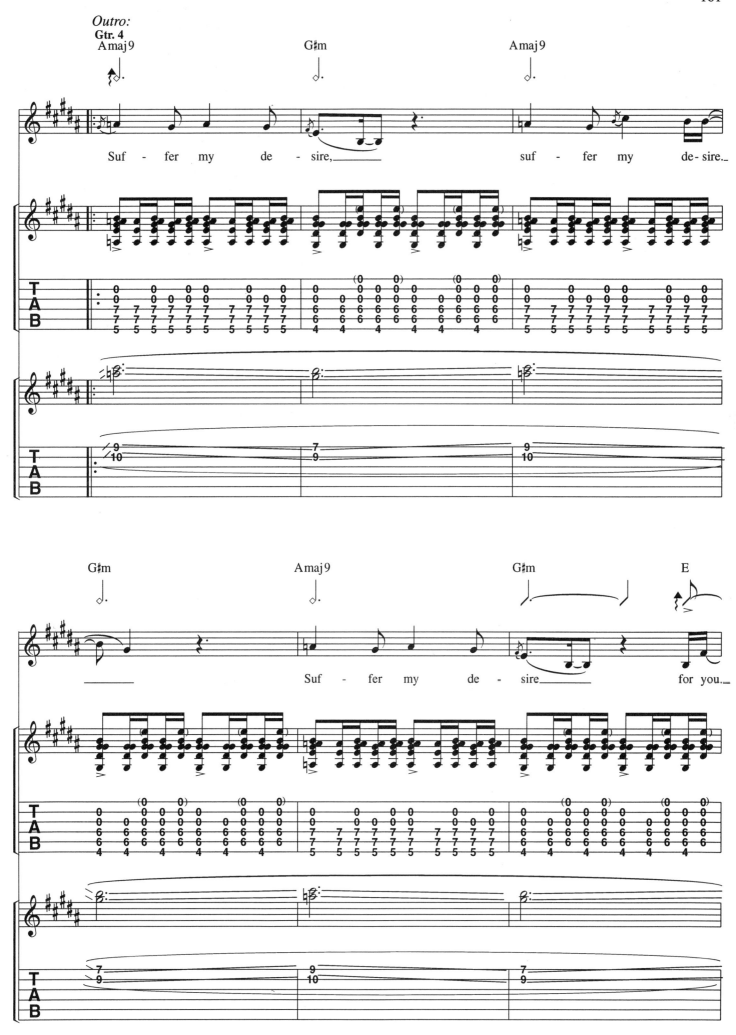

162

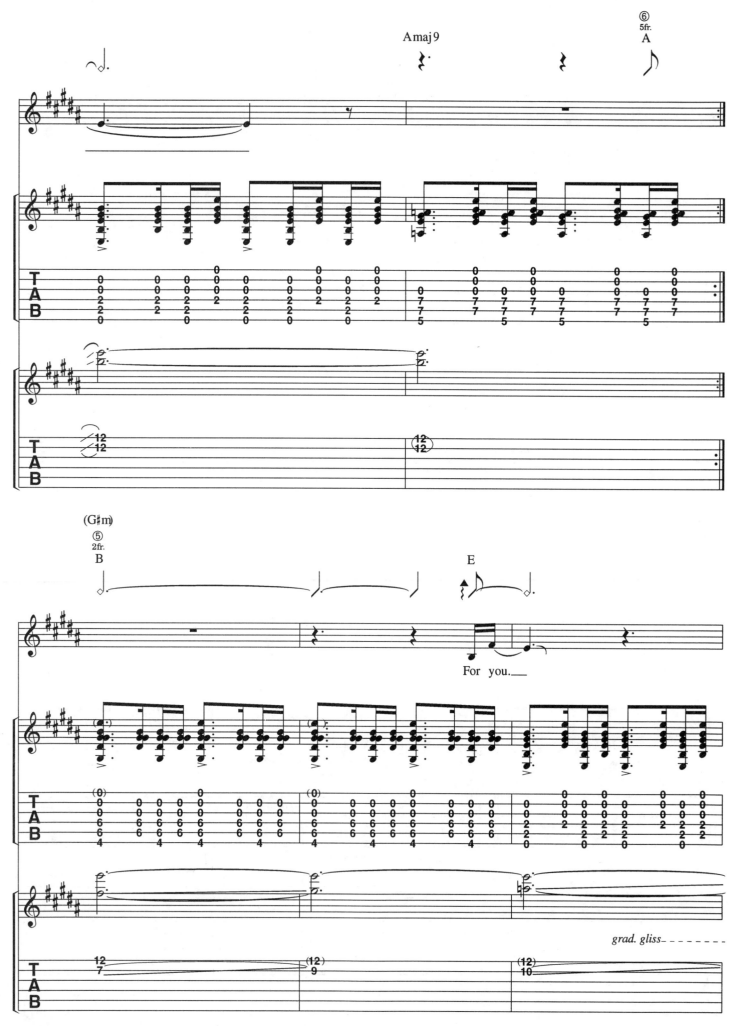

For you.___

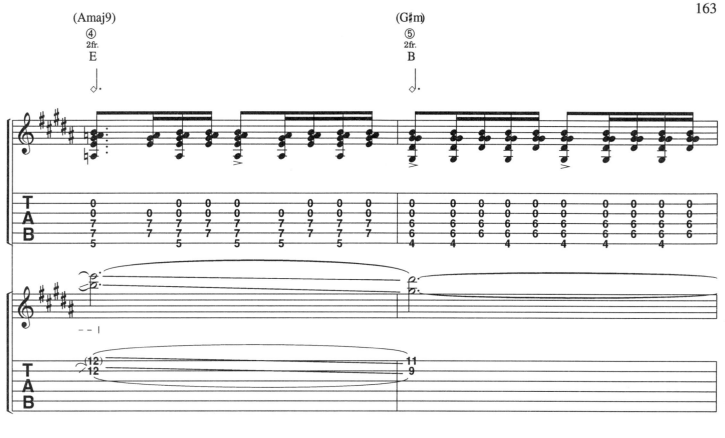

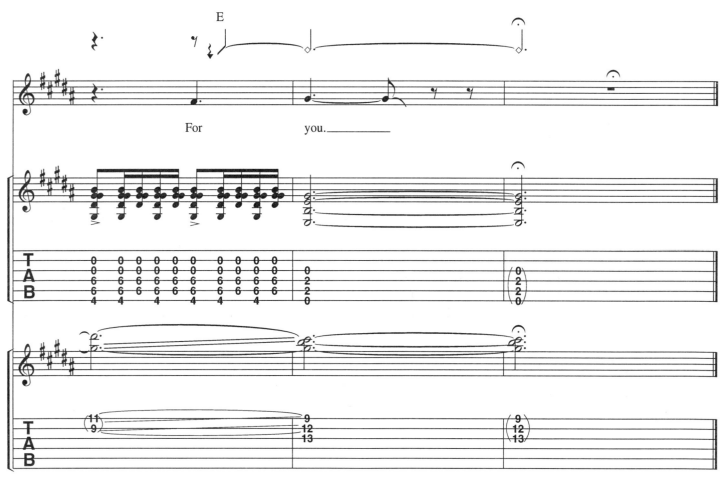

Verse 2:
I steal a kiss from her, sleeping shadow moves.
'Cause I'll always miss her wherever she goes.
And I'll always need her more
Than she could ever need me.
I need someone to ease my mind.

Verse 3:
She comes to me like an angel out of time.
As I play the part of a saint on my knees.
There are some things I'll live without.
But I want you to know that I need you right now.

1979

Emaj7

E

F#m7sus

B

E5

Emaj7
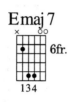

E5

F#7(11)

A(9)

B5

C#m

E

1979

Words and Music by
BILLY CORGAN

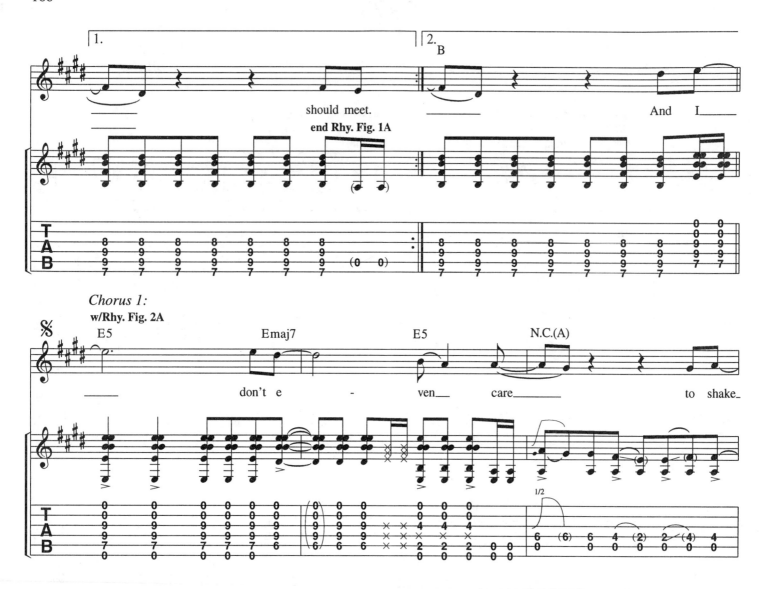

Chorus 1:

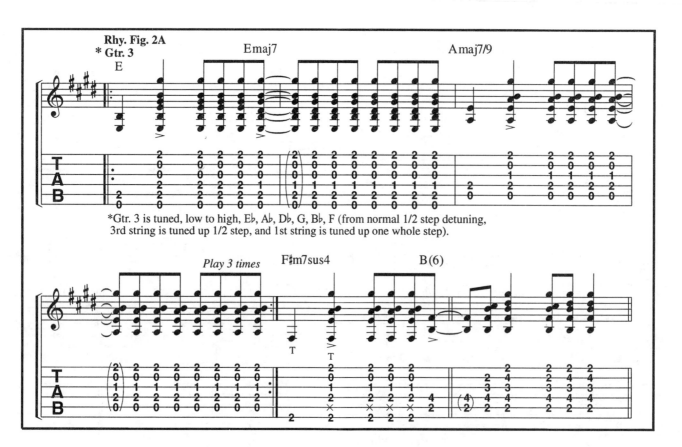

*Gtr. 3 is tuned, low to high, E♭, A♭, D♭, G, B♭, F (from normal 1/2 step detuning, 3rd string is tuned up 1/2 step, and 1st string is tuned up one whole step).

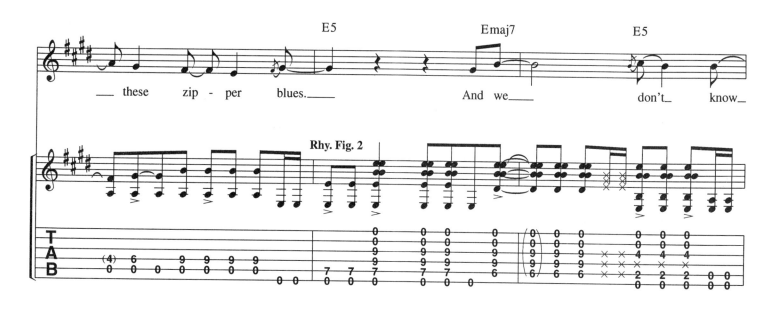

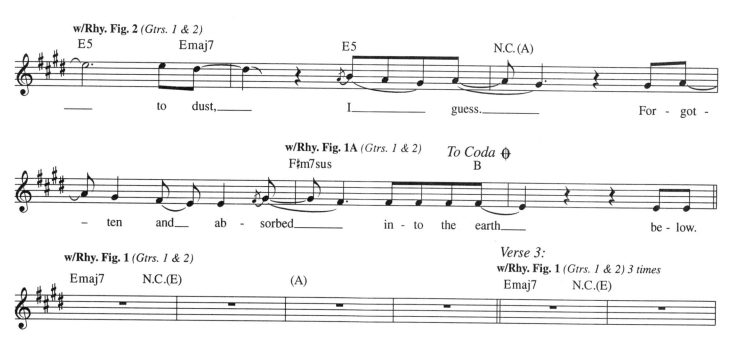

168

1979 - 7 - 4
PG9602

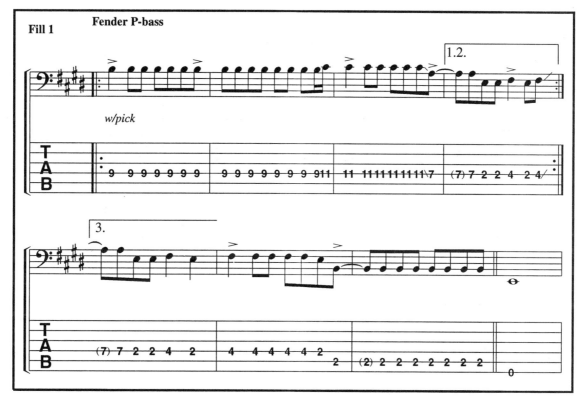

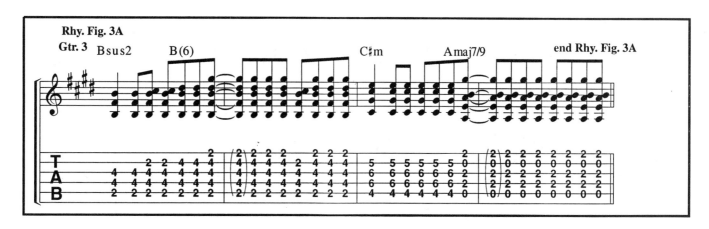

170

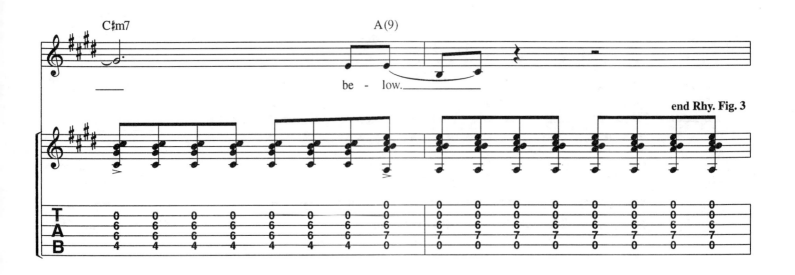

be - low.___ end Rhy. Fig. 3

w/Rhy. Figs. 3 *(Gtrs. 1 & 2)* **& 3A** *(Gtr. 3) 2 times*

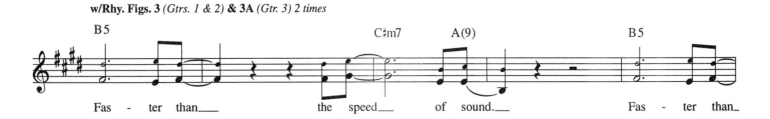

Fas - ter than___ the speed___ of sound.___ Fas - ter than_

w/Rhy. Fig. 4

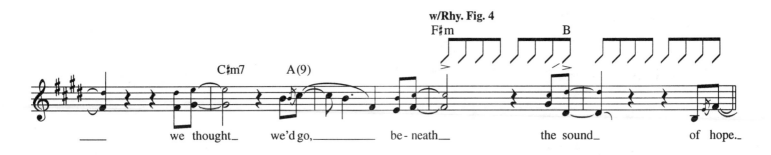

___ we thought_ we'd go,_____ be - neath_ the sound_ of hope._

Rhy. Fig. 4

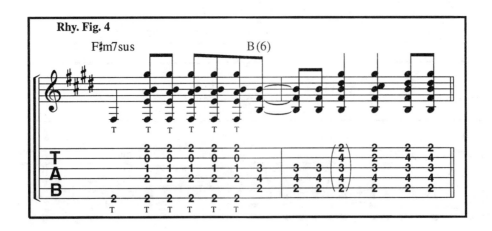

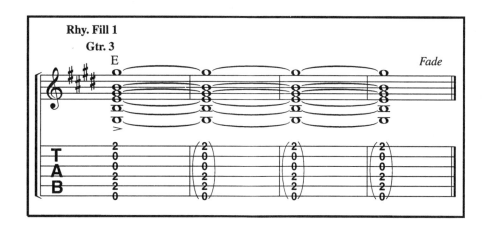

TALES OF A SCORCHED EARTH

E5

G5

A5

B5

D5

E

A5

C5

F#5

G#5

A5

B5

C#5

Am

Bm/A

A

D/A

TALES OF A SCORCHED EARTH

Words and Music by
BILLY CORGAN

All gtrs. tune down whole step.
Music sounds one whole-step lower than written.

Moderately fast rock ♩ = 128

A5

1. Fare - well, good - night, last one out turn out the lights and

Verse:
w/Rhy. Fig. 2 *(Gtr. 1) 2 times, simile*

E5   G5 A5 E5   B5 D5   E   G5A5E5   B5 D5   E   G5A5 E5   B5 D5   E   G5A5 E5   B5D5

let me be.__ Let me die in - side.__ Let me know the__ way__ through this world of__ hate__ in__ you..

N.C.   A5

2. 'Cause the

Gtr. 1

𝄋 *Verse:*
w/Rhy. Fig. 2 *(Gtr. 1) 2 times, simile*

E5   G5 A5   E5   B5 D5   E   G5 A5   E5   B5 D5

die   is__   cast__   and   the   bitch   is   back.__   And

4. *See additional lyrics*

E   G5 A5   E5   B5   D5   E   G5 A5   E5   B5 D5

we're   all__   dead,__   yeah,__   we're   all__   dead._____

2nd vox: In - side__

Tales Of A Scorched Earth - 7 - 5
PG9602

178

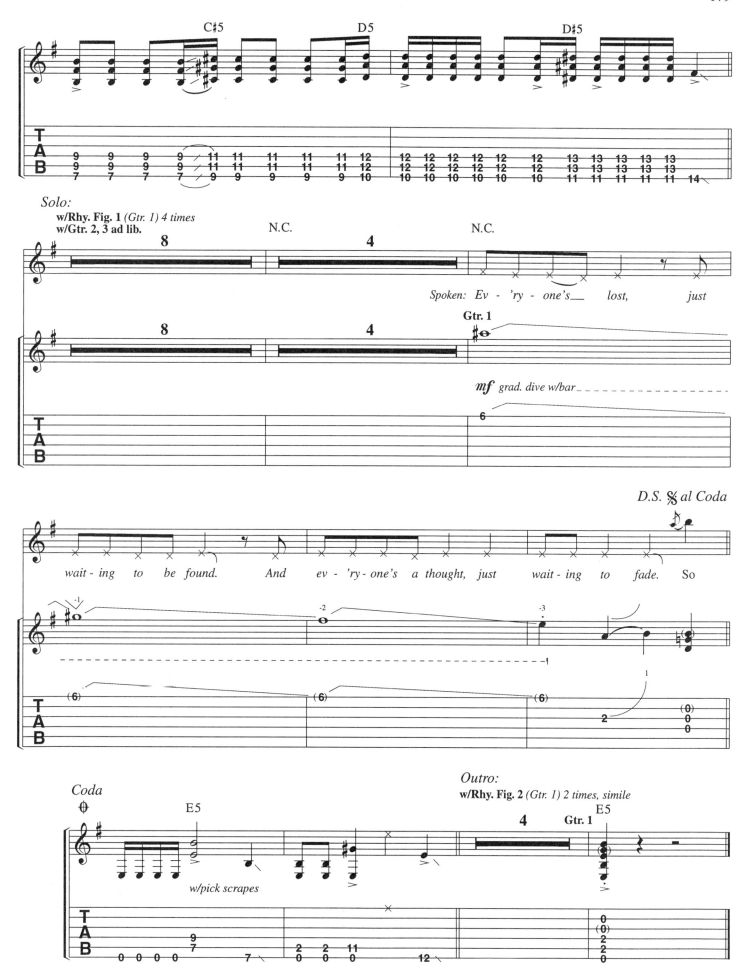

Verse 4:
So fuck it all 'cause I don't care.
So what, somehow, somewhere we dared
To try to dare, to dare for a little more. . .

THRU THE EYES OF RUBY

E

G

D

F#

A

A#

B

F#sus

Mellon Collie Reprise, Gtr. 1 capo 3.

Gm

Bb

F

Eb

Cm

Ab

THRU THE EYES OF RUBY

Words and Music by
BILLY CORGAN

Tune all gtrs. down 1/2 step:
⑥ = E♭   ③ = G♭
⑤ = A♭   ② = B♭
④ = D♭   ① = E♭

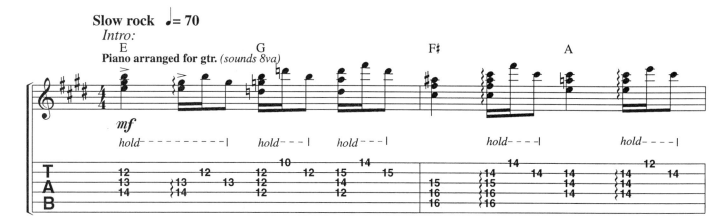

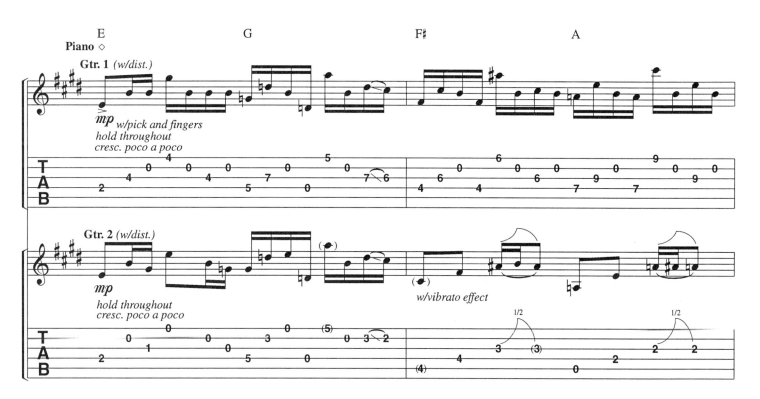

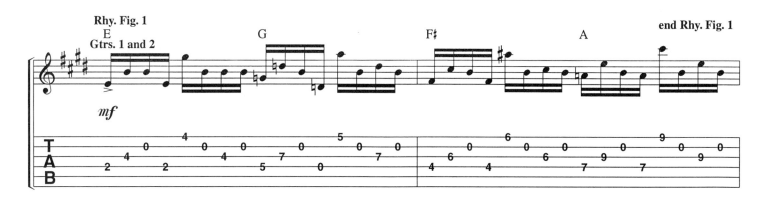

Thru The Eyes Of Ruby - 13 - 1
PG9602

182

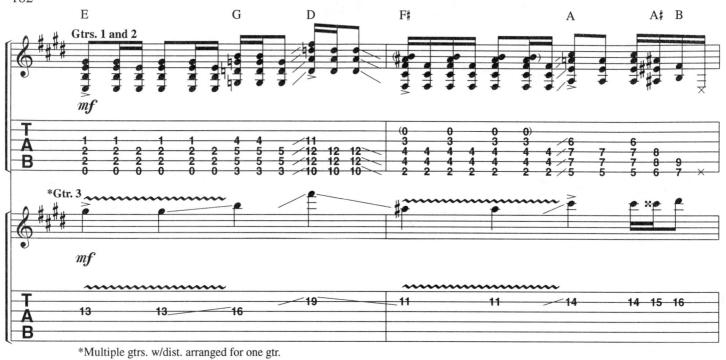

*Multiple gtrs. w/dist. arranged for one gtr.

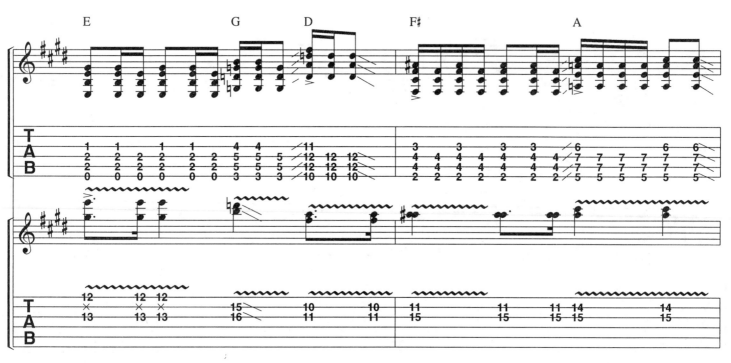

Thru The Eyes Of Ruby - 13 - 2
PG9602

Breath - ing un - der - wa - ter___

Gtrs. 1 and 2 *(w/flanger effect)*

mf
hold throughout

Chorus:

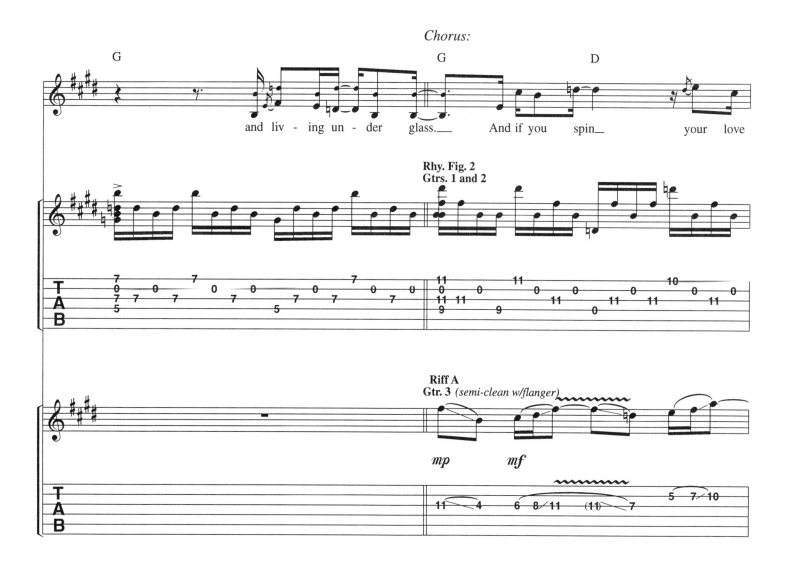

and liv - ing un - der glass.___ And if you spin___ your love

Rhy. Fig. 2
Gtrs. 1 and 2

Riff A
Gtr. 3 *(semi-clean w/flanger)*

mp   *mf*

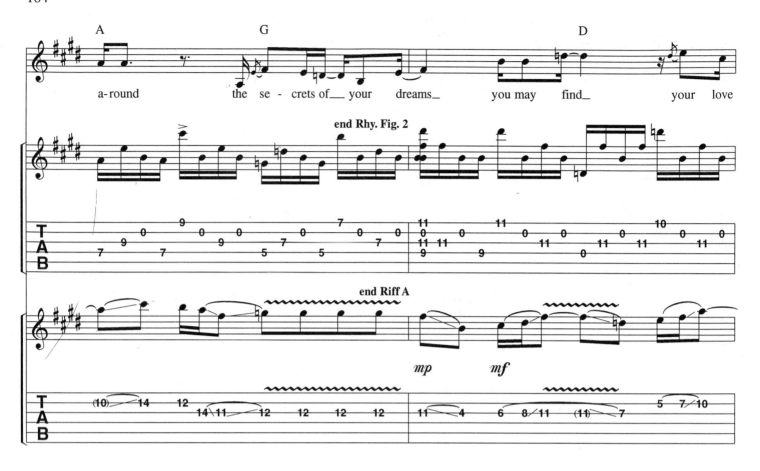

a-round   the se - crets of__ your   dreams__   you may   find__   your love

end Rhy. Fig. 2

end Riff A

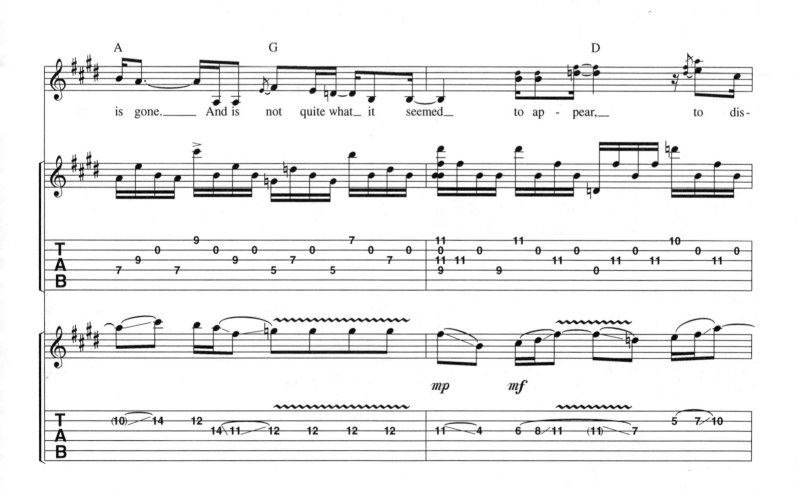

is gone.___ And is   not   quite what__ it   seemed__   to ap - pear,__   to dis-

ap-pear___ be-neath all your dark-est fears.___

Thru The Eyes Of Ruby - 13 - 5
PG9602

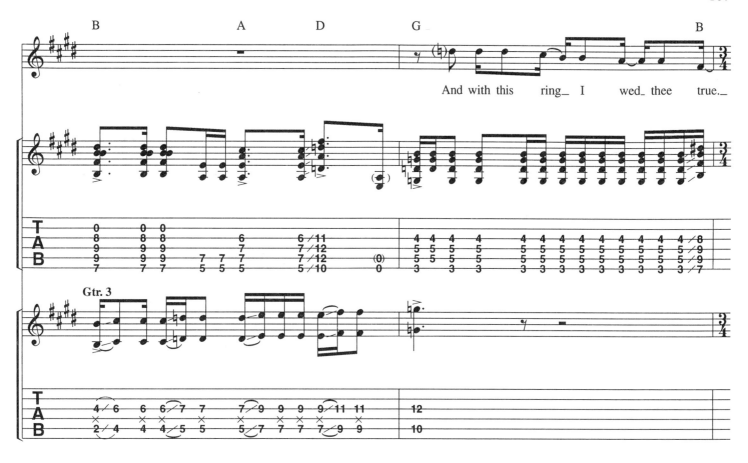

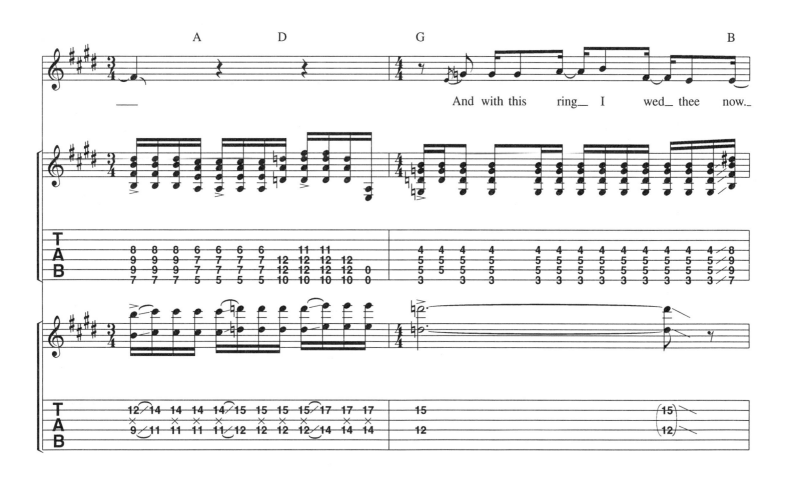

91

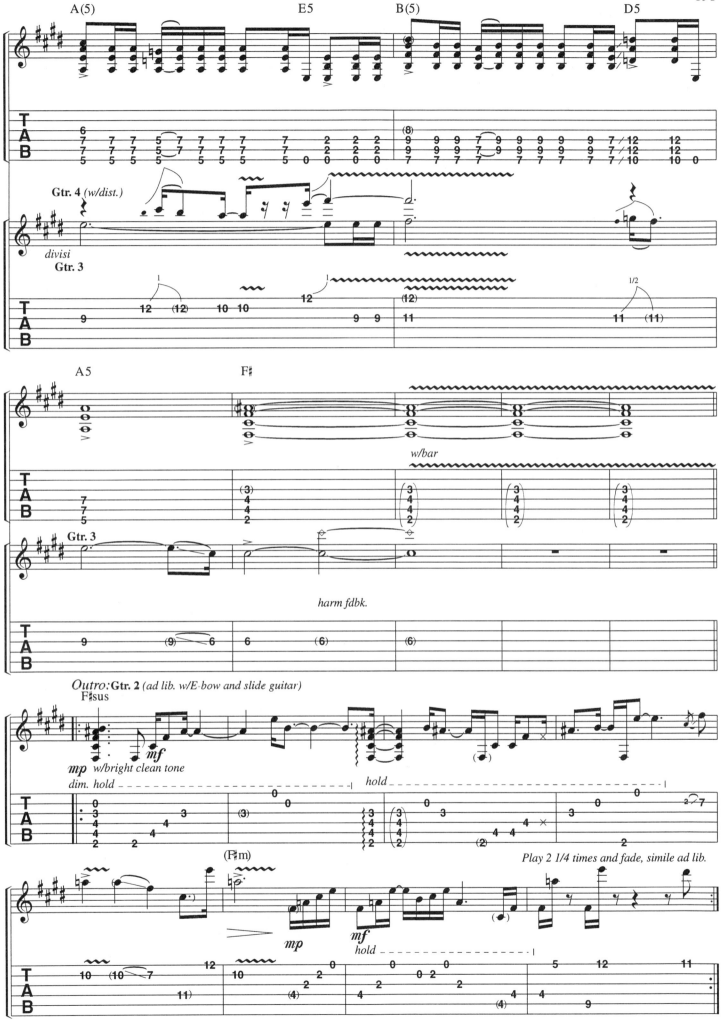

Thru The Eyes Of Ruby - 13 - 11
PG9602

"Mellon Collie Reprise"
Tune gtrs. down 1/2 step:

*The number zero in tablature represents capoed open string.

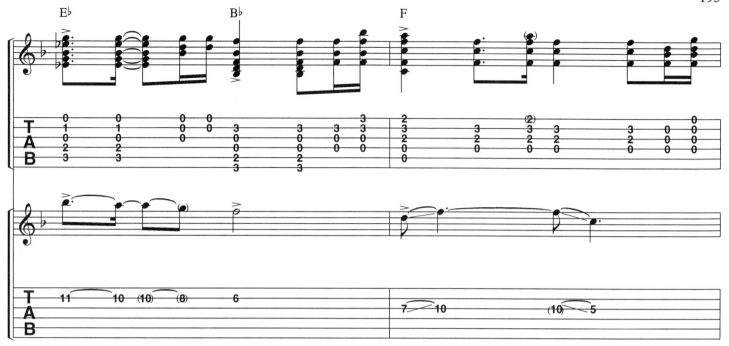

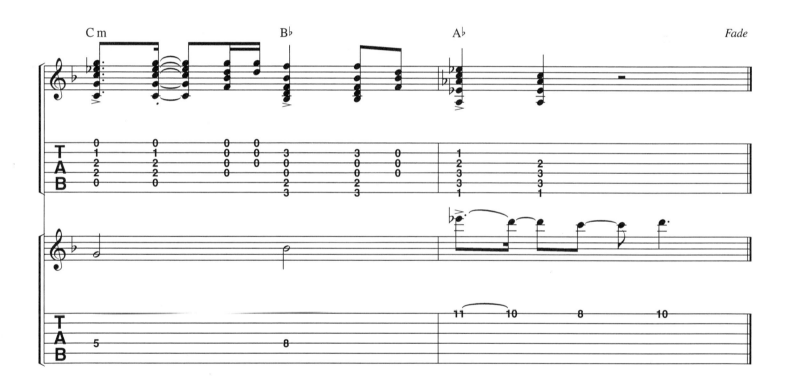

Verse 3:
Your strength is my weakness,
Your weakness my hate.
My love for you just can't explain
Why we're forever frozen.
Forever beautiful,
Forever lost inside ourselves…

STUMBLEINE

This is another song in which Billy uses simple chord shapes (mostly power chords) in combination with open strings to produce more complex and interesting chord sounds.

D

7fr.

Dsus

8fr.

Bm

7fr.

A(5)

5fr.

G5

A7

5fr.

Csus2

8fr.

Asus

5fr.

Dsus

10fr.

C

8fr.

STUMBLEINE

Words and Music by
BILLY CORGAN

Tune gtr. down 1/2 step:
⑥ = E♭ ③ = G♭
⑤ = A♭ ② = B♭
④ = D♭ ① = E♭

Slowly ♩ = 62
Verse:

1. Bore-dom's in the bath-room, shak-ing out the loose teeth.

Sal-ly in the stir-rups, claim-ing her own des-ti-ny.

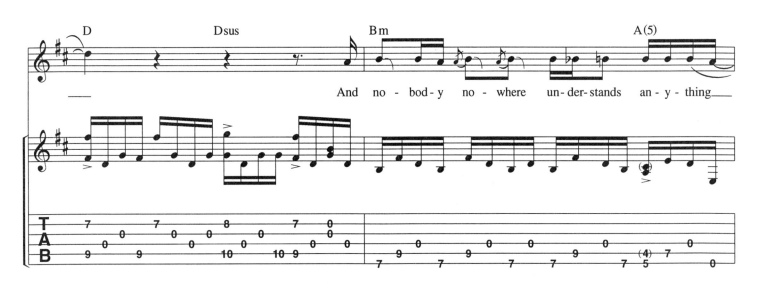

And no-bod-y no-where un-der-stands an-y-thing

Stumbleine - 4 - 1
PG9602

196

198

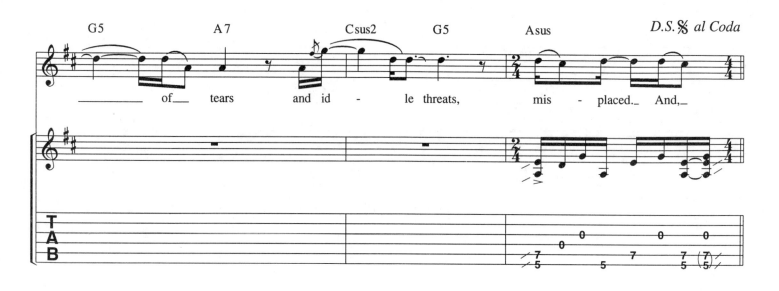

Stumbleine - 4 - 4
PG9602

X.Y.U.

Words and Music by
BILLY CORGAN

Tune all gtrs. down 1/2 step:
⑥ = E♭ ③ = G♭
⑤ = A♭ ② = B♭
④ = D♭ ① = E♭

F#5   E5   G5

Moderate rock ♩ = 114

Intro:
N.C.
*Gtrs. 1 & 2 (w/dist.)

mf

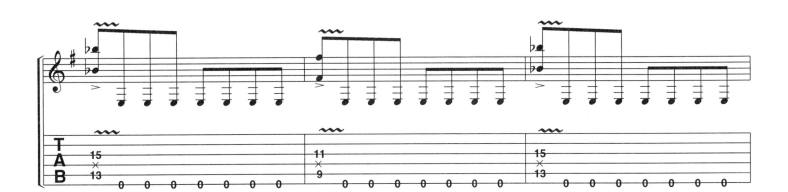

*Two gtrs. arranged for one.

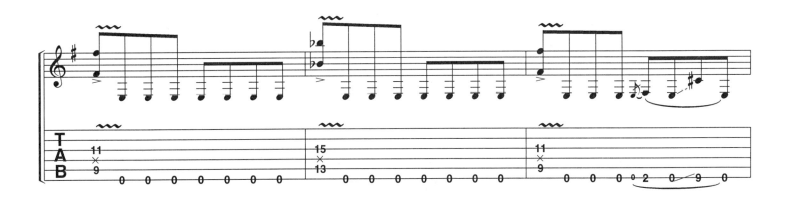

f

X.Y.U. - 8 - 1
PG9602

Verse 1:

1. She did - n't wan - na be, she did - n't wan - na know.
2. *See additional lyrics*

Rhy. Fig. 1

mf
poco dim.

She could - n't run a - way 'cause she was cra - zy. **end Rhy. Fig. 1**

w/Rhy. Fig. 1 *(Gtr. 1, dbld)*

She gave it all a-way, she saw her ba-by break. And in the air it hung that she was dull ra-zors.

202

X.Y.U. - 8 - 4
PG9602

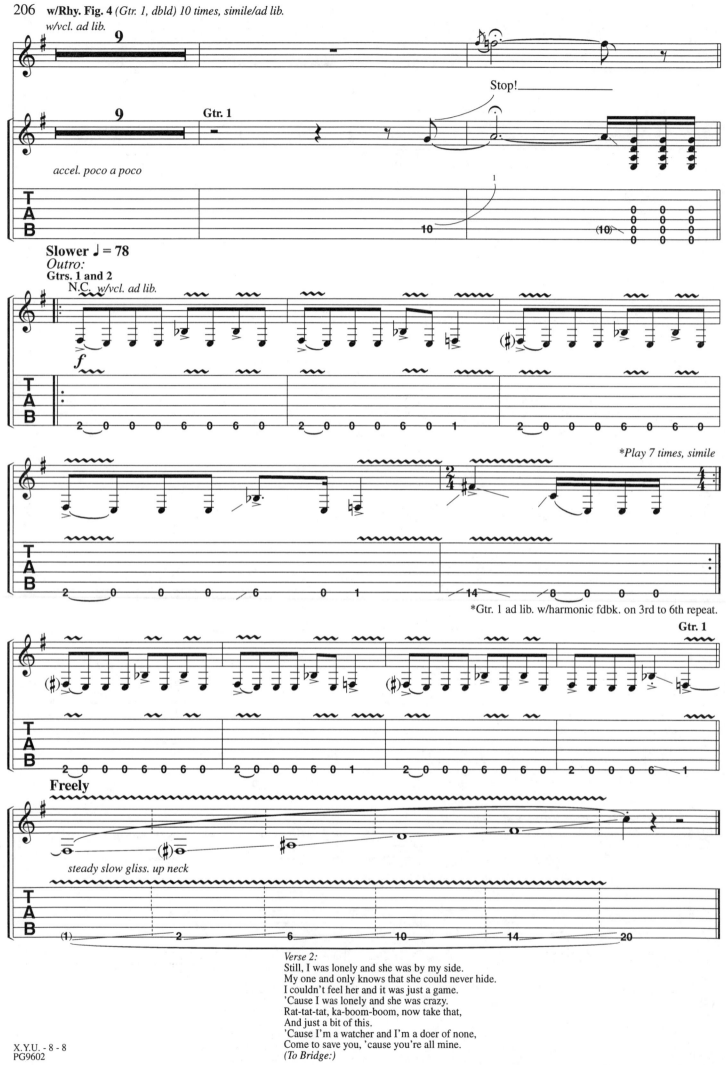

Verse 2:
Still, I was lonely and she was by my side.
My one and only knows that she could never hide.
I couldn't feel her and it was just a game.
'Cause I was lonely and she was crazy.
Rat-tat-tat, ka-boom-boom, now take that,
And just a bit of this.
'Cause I'm a watcher and I'm a doer of none,
Come to save you, 'cause you're all mine.
(To Bridge:)

WE ONLY COME OUT AT NIGHT

Words and Music by
BILLY CORGAN

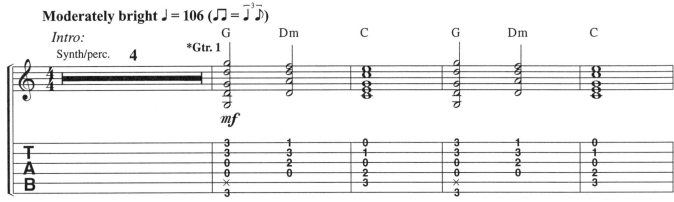

*Autoharp arranged for gtr.

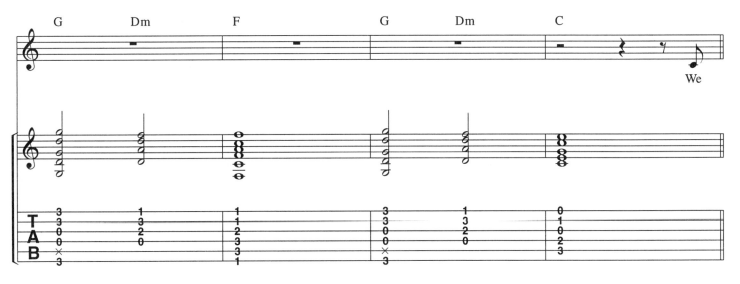

Chorus:
(Guitar cont. simile throughout.)

on-ly come out at night, we on-ly come out at

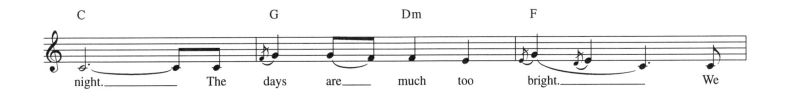

night. The days are much too bright. We

3. And once_ a - gain,_____ now,_____ you'll pre - tend_____ to know_ that,

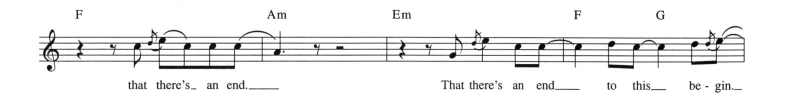

that there's_ an end._____ That there's an end____ to this__ be - gin._

_____ It will help____ you sleep_ at night.__ It will make____ it seem__ that right_

_ is al - ways right._____ Al - right?_____ We

D.S. ℀ al Coda

Coda

✠ *Outro:*

Play 2 1/2 times and fade

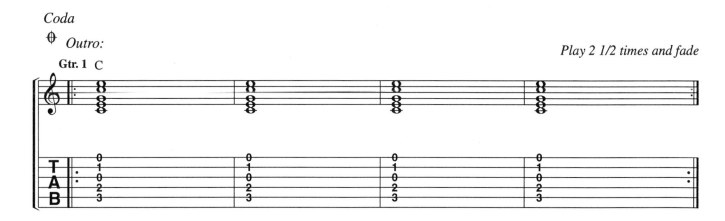

Verse 2:
I walk alone, I walk alone to find the way home.
I'm on my own, I'm on my own to see the ways,
That I can't help the days.
You will make it home o.k.
I know you can, and you can…

BEAUTIFUL

Words and Music by
BILLY CORGAN

Beau - ti - ful, you're

beau - ti - ful, as beau - ti - ful as the sun.

212

Won - der - ful, it's won - der - ful__ to know that you're_ just like I._____

Chorus:
w/Riff D *(4 times); on D.S., substitute Riff B for Riff D*

And I'm sure you know__ me__ well,__ as I'm sure you don't.__

___ But you just can't_____ tell__

To Coda ⊕   **w/Riff D** *(1st bar only); on D.S., w/Riff B (1st bar only)*

who you'll love and who you__ won't,__ no,__ no, who you'll love and who you__ won't.

Riff D
Piano arr. for gtr.
8va

LILY (MY ONE AND ONLY)

Words and Music by
BILLY CORGAN

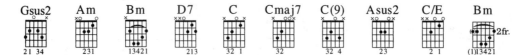

Tune all gtrs. down 1/2 step:
⑥ = E♭ ③ = G♭
⑤ = A♭ ② = B♭
④ = D♭ ① = E♭

Moderately ♩ = 98 (♫ = ♩³♪)   **Rhy. Fig. 1**
Gtr. 1 *(Electric w/clean tone)*

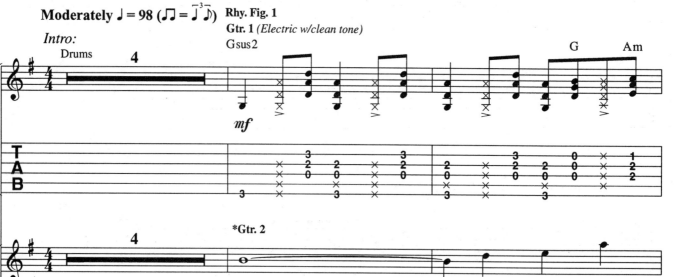

*Keyboard arranged for gtr.

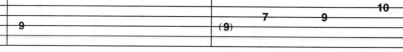

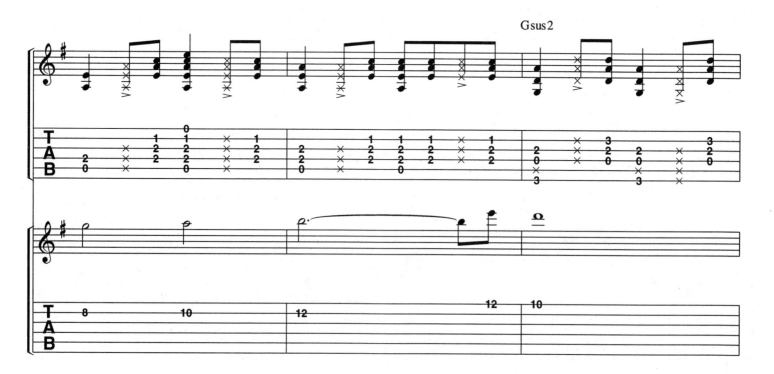

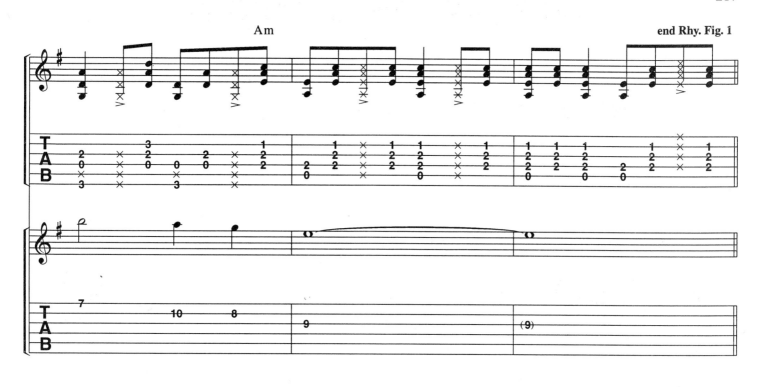

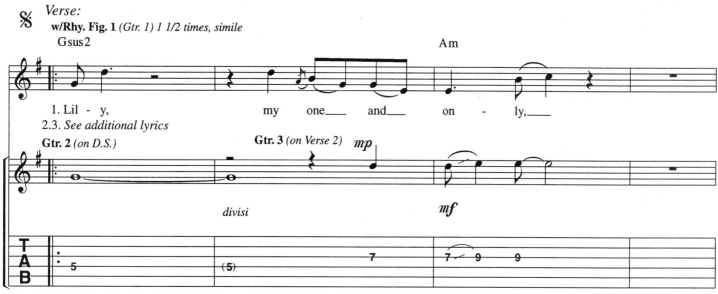

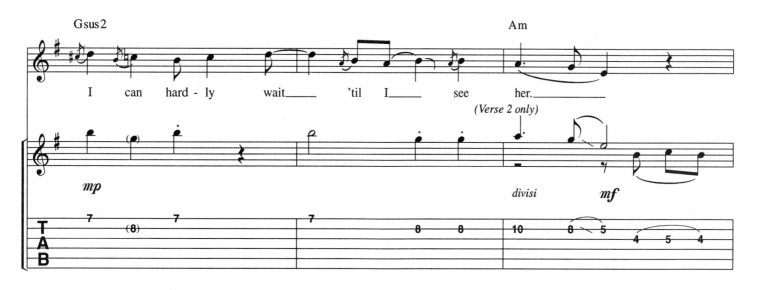

Lily (My One and Only) - 6 - 2
PG9602

218

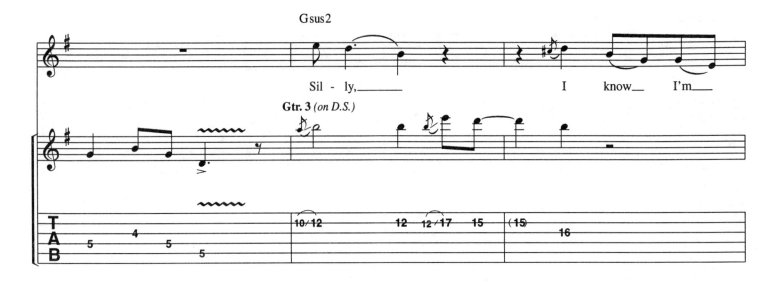

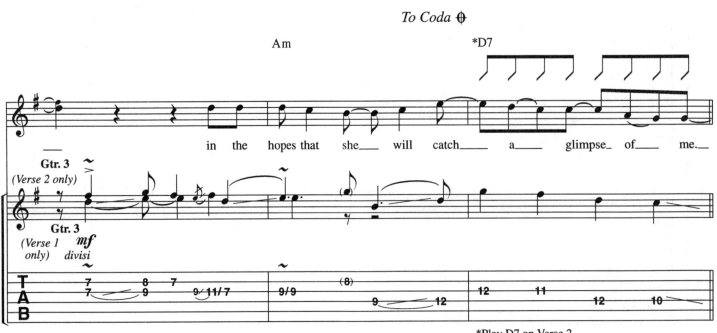

*Play D7 on Verse 2.

Lily (My One and Only) - 6 - 3
PG9602

Lily (My One and Only) - 6 - 5
PG9602

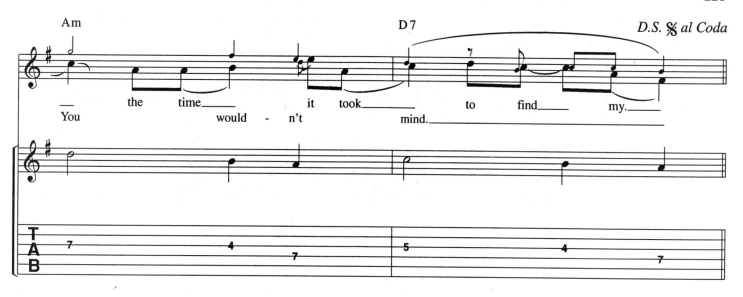

Verse 2:
Lily, my one and only.
Love is in my heart and in your eyes.
Will she or won't she want him,
No one knows for sure.
But an officer is knocking at my door…

Verse 3:
My Lily, my one and only.
I can hardly wait 'til I see her.
Oh, Lily, I know you love me,
'Cause as they're dragging me away,
I swear I saw her raise her hand and wave
(Goodbye).

BY STARLIGHT

Dsus2

Dmaj9

Am

G

Dmaj7

Em

A

A(9)

D

Bm

Gmaj7

BY STARLIGHT

Words and Music by
BILLY CORGAN

*Tune all gtrs. down 1 whole step. Song will
sound one whole-step lower than written.

Moderately ♩ = 106

224

By Starlight - 9 - 2
PG9602

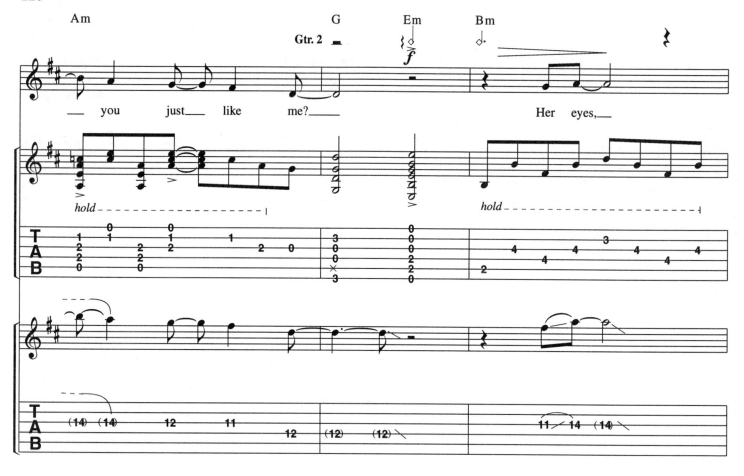

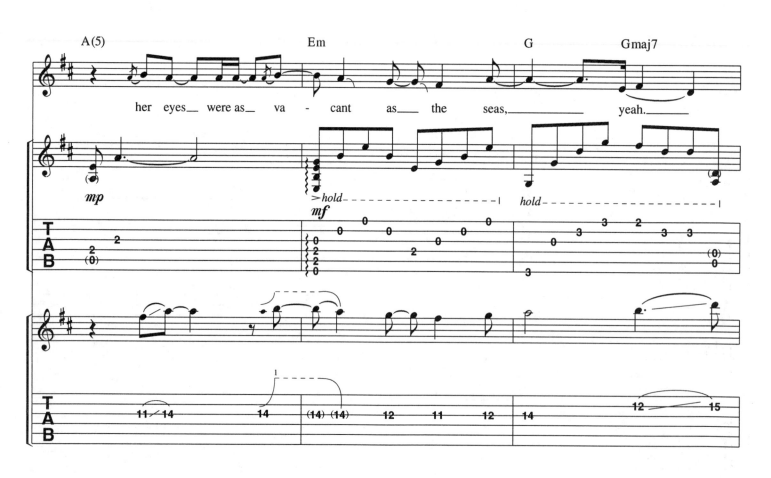

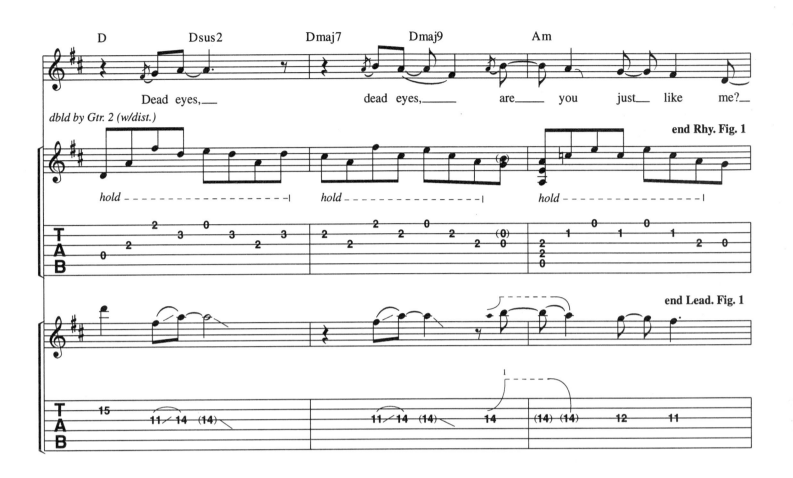

230

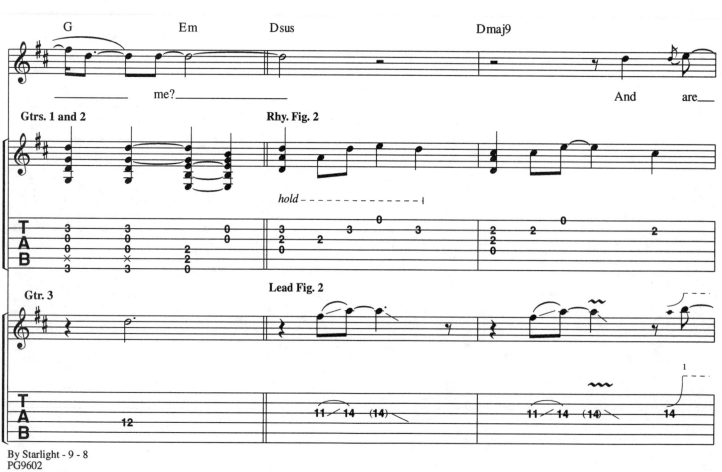

By Starlight - 9 - 8
PG9602

FAREWELL AND GOODNIGHT

This song uses the same altered tuning as "Muzzle". Compared to standard tuning, the ② string is tuned down a whole-step to "A" (then the whole guitar is tuned down a half-step).

C6

Fmaj7

Gsus

F

Am7

D9

Em(♯5)

Gtr. 3 (standard tuning)

Am

D

F

G

C

FAREWELL AND GOODNIGHT

Words and Music by
JAMES IHA and BILLY CORGAN

Tune Gtrs. 1 and 2 down 1/2 step:
⑥ = E♭ ③ = G♭
⑤ = A♭ ② = A♭ –Tune 2nd string down 1 1/2 steps:
④ = D♭ ① = E♭

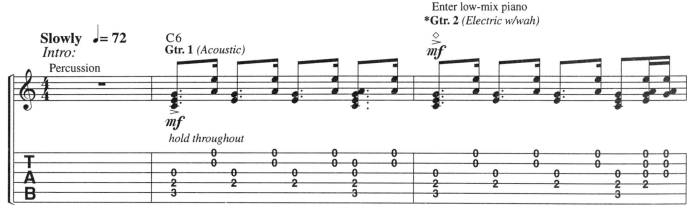

*Rock wah back and forth in 8ths throughout.
Play same voicings as Gtr. 1.

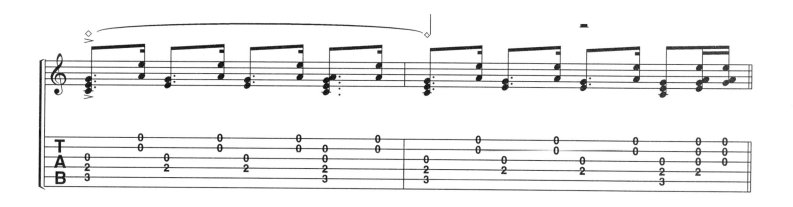

Good - night, to ev - 'ry lit - tle hour___ that you

Farewell And Goodnight - 6 - 1
PG9602

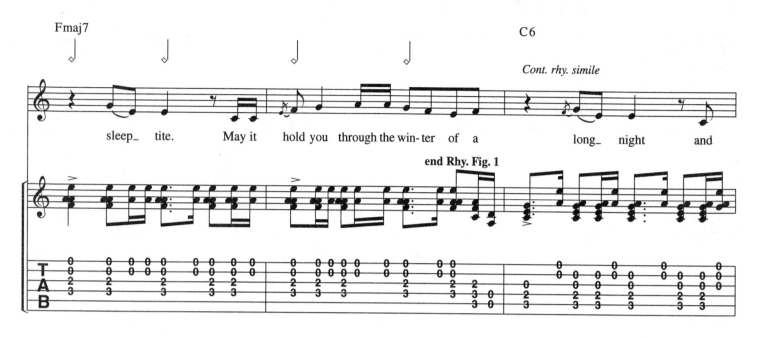

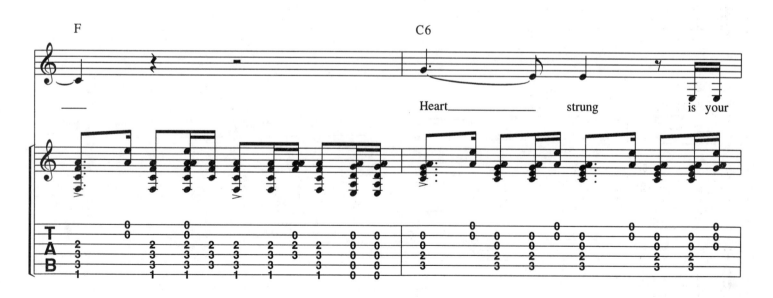

236

Farewell And Goodnight - 6 - 4
PG9602

Chorus:

w/Rhy. **Fig. 2** *(Gtrs. 1 and 2) simile*

Good - night, my love,_____ to ev-'ry hour_____ in ev-'ry___ day.___

___ Good - night, al - ways,_____ to all that's pure___

___ that's in your heart._____

Outro:

w/Rhy. **Fig. 2** *(Gtr. 1) 1st 3 bars, simile and fade*

Piano   Band tacet

*Gtr. 3

mf
dim.
hold throughout

*Tune down 1/2 step - piano arranged here for gtr.
Sounds octave higher than written.

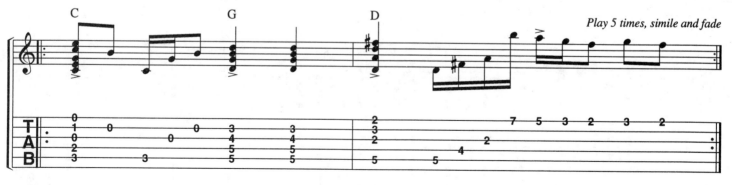

Play 5 times, simile and fade

GUITAR TAB GLOSSARY **

TABLATURE EXPLANATION

READING TABLATURE: Tablature illustrates the six strings of the guitar. Notes and chords are indicated by the placement of fret numbers on a given string(s).

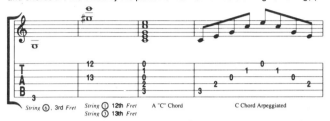

String ⑥, 3rd Fret   String ① 12th Fret   A "C" Chord   C Chord Arpeggiated
String ③ 13th Fret

BENDING NOTES

HALF STEP: Play the note and bend string one half step.*

WHOLE STEP: Play the note and bend string one whole step.

WHOLE STEP AND A HALF: Play the note and bend string a whole step and a half.

SLIGHT BEND (Microtone): Play the note and bend string slightly to the equivalent of half a fret.

PREBEND (Ghost Bend): Bend to the specified note, before the string is picked.

PREBEND AND RELEASE: Bend the string, play it, then release to the original note.

REVERSE BEND: Play the already-bent string, then immediately drop it down to the fretted note.

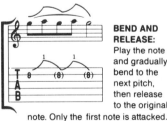

BEND AND RELEASE: Play the note and gradually bend to the next pitch, then release to the original note. Only the first note is attacked.

*A half step is the smallest interval in Western music; it is equal to one fret. A whole step equals two frets.

UNISON BEND: Play both notes and immediately bend the lower note to the same pitch as the higher note.

DOUBLE NOTE BEND: Play both notes and immediately bend both strings simultaneously.

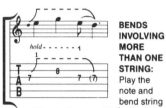

BENDS INVOLVING MORE THAN ONE STRING: Play the note and bend string while playing an additional note (or notes) on another string(s). Upon release, relieve pressure from additional note(s), causing original note to sound alone.

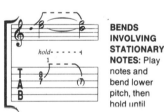

BENDS INVOLVING STATIONARY NOTES: Play notes and bend lower pitch, then hold until release begins (indicated at the point where line becomes solid).

TREMOLO BAR

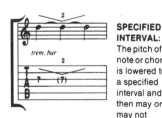

SPECIFIED INTERVAL: The pitch of a note or chord is lowered to a specified interval and then may or may not return to the original pitch. The activity of the tremolo bar is graphically represented by peaks and valleys.

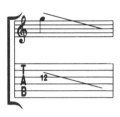

UN-SPECIFIED INTERVAL: The pitch of a note or a chord is lowered to an unspecified interval.

HARMONICS

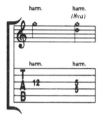

NATURAL HARMONIC: A finger of the fret hand lightly touches the note or notes indicated in the tab and is played by the pick hand.

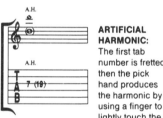

ARTIFICIAL HARMONIC: The first tab number is fretted, then the pick hand produces the harmonic by using a finger to lightly touch the same string at the second tab number (in parenthesis) and is then picked by another finger.

ARTIFICIAL "PINCH" HARMONIC: A note is fretted as indicated by the tab, then the pick hand produces the harmonic by squeezing the pick firmly while using the tip of the index finger in the pick attack. If parenthesis are found around the fretted note, it does not sound. No parenthesis means both the fretted note and A.H. are heard simultaneously.

RHYTHM SLASHES

STRUM INDICA-TIONS: Strum with indicated rhythm.

The chord voicings are found on the first page of the transcription underneath the song title.

INDICATING SINGLE NOTES USING RHYTHM SLASHES: Very often single notes are incorporated into a rhythm part. The note name is indicated above the rhythm slash with a fret number and a string indication.

ARTICULATIONS

HAMMER ON: Play lower note, then "hammer on" to higher note with another finger. Only the first note is attacked.

LEFT HAND HAMMER: Hammer on the first note played on each string with the left hand.

PULL OFF: Play higher note, then "pull off" to lower note with another finger. Only the first note is attacked.

FRET-BOARD TAPPING: "Tap" onto the note indicated by + with a finger of the pick hand, then pull off to the following note held by the fret hand.

TAP SLIDE: Same as fretboard tapping, but the tapped note is slid randomly up the fretboard, then pulled off to the following note.

BEND AND TAP TECHNIQUE: Play note and bend to specified interval. While holding bend, tap onto note indicated.

LEGATO SLIDE: Play note and slide to the following note. (Only first note is attacked).

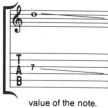

LONG GLISSAN-DO: Play note and slide in specified direction for the full value of the note.

SHORT GLISSAN-DO: Play note for its full value and slide in specified direction at the last possible moment.

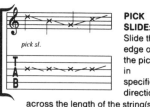
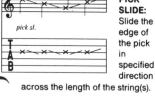

PICK SLIDE: Slide the edge of the pick in specified direction across the length of the string(s).

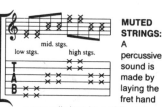

MUTED STRINGS: A percussive sound is made by laying the fret hand across all six strings while pick hand strikes specified area (low, mid, high strings).

PALM MUTE: The note or notes are muted by the palm of the pick hand by lightly touching the string(s) near the bridge.

TREMOLO PICKING: The note or notes are picked as fast as possible.

TRILL: Hammer on and pull off consecutively and as fast as possible between the original note and the grace note.

ACCENT: Notes or chords are to be played with added emphasis.

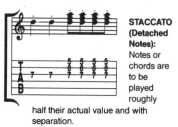

STACCATO (Detached Notes): Notes or chords are to be played roughly half their actual value and with separation.

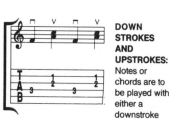

DOWN STROKES AND UPSTROKES: Notes or chords are to be played with either a downstroke (⊓) or upstroke (⋁) of the pick.

VIBRATO: The pitch of a note is varied by a rapid shaking of the fret hand finger, wrist, and forearm.